MY VOICE

My Voice
Tells The Story

by

MYRTLE BEGGS
(née Bradford)

JOHN RITCHIE LTD
CHRISTIAN PUBLICATIONS

40 Beansburn, Kilmarnock, Scotland

ISBN-13: 978 1 910513 44 6

Copyright © 2015 by John Ritchie Ltd.
40 Beansburn, Kilmarnock, Scotland

www.ritchiechristianmedia.co.uk

Typeset by John Ritchie Ltd., Kilmarnock
Printed by Bell & Bain Ltd., Glasgow

Contents

Introduction

My aim in writing this book is to allow you to come with me down through the many years of joy and sorrow that I have experienced in my life. I also write this in admiration of and appreciation to both my parents, Hugh and May Bradford, now deceased. Both my parents were saved by God's grace long before I was born. However, even though I had saved parents, this was no guarantee that I too would be saved and join them in Heaven.

At a young age I escaped death from drowning. God overruled in those circumstances at that time. At the age of sixteen years I made a false profession of faith in Christ. I was deceived by Satan, the devil himself, for four years, who led me to believe that I was on my way to Heaven.

After leaving home to take up a nursing profession, I met and married Martin and settled into our first home as husband and wife. In 1966 our first little girl was born and I had many sleepless nights. I recall one night when, after settling down for, as I thought, a good night's sleep, suddenly the bedroom lit up with lightning, and thunder was heard in the distance. A very large bang took place and the lights went out - our home had been struck by the lightning, leaving a great trail of destruction. I was totally shocked. God used this instance to speak to me and at that time my thoughts were drawn to go around my own foundation. What was I depending on to take me to Heaven? It was at this point that I began to have doubts as to whether I was really saved at all. I knew no one could answer this, only myself. A few weeks later, after coming home from a gospel meeting, I made up my mind that, if salvation was to be had, it was now or never.

The date was the 21st November 1966; the time, 1:05am. I was very anxious to get this great matter of salvation settled and just in a moment, as I was about to give this whole thing up, I realised that salvation was by faith in Christ and what was accomplished on the cross of Calvary for a sinner like me. The hymn became real to me:

> Calvary's cross the only refuge!
> Calvary's cross the only plea!
> Calvary's cross! O, blessed shelter!
> On it God's salvation see!
>
> Albert Midlane (1825 – 1909)

I knew I was saved, my sins were gone. Salvation is obtained through faith.

When I reached the age of fifty years old, my faith in Christ was to be tested. I was diagnosed with throat cancer. This was to change my way of living, as I lost my voice through extensive surgery in the Royal Victoria Hospital, Belfast. Many deep trials and disappointments were to follow, trying to come to terms with total loss of speech. However, with the help and care I received from my family, and the prayers of many, many Christians, both at home and in many other countries throughout the world, lifting my every need to the God of all comfort, I was able to maintain a positive attitude.

I owe a special thanks to my consultant, Mr Primrose, and all the team of doctors, nursing staff, speech therapist and other members of staff, too numerous to mention, in the ENT Ward 29 of the Royal Victoria Hospital, and also to the staff and doctors of Dromore Doctors Surgery, not forgetting the great team of Macmillan nurses that attended me in a professional manner.

I would like to express my sincere thanks to those who took of their time and effort to provide information and recollections, those who sifted and sorted and took on the task of proof-reading. Also I am indebted to my daughter Sharon who undertook the onerous task of typing up my book.

I must give the glory to my Saviour, Who brought me through some of the darkest days of my life. It was these words, found in the Holy Scriptures, which kept me going: "The eternal God is thy refuge, and underneath are the everlasting arms" (Deuteronomy 33:27). I can say with confidence, "To God be the glory, great things He hath done." He brought me through my first year, which was a big challenge for me, trying to use my artificial servox, my only means of speech.

It has been a hard struggle for all of us and now, twenty years on, because the Lord has preserved me thus far, I am here to tell my story. I pray that it will be a big encouragement to any readers who are passing through trials and difficulties.

God's word says, "Trust in the Lord with all thine heart; and lean not unto thine own understanding. In all thy ways acknowledge Him and He shall direct thy paths" (Proverbs 3:5,6).

My voice tells the story.

Chapter 1

My Home and Upbringing

I was born on the 2nd December 1944, into a home where both my parents were born again Christians. I was the youngest of a family of five, with two older brothers and two older sisters. We were brought up on a farm in the townland of Shanaghan, Katesbridge, and like many others in our area we had very little luxuries. No electricity, just a Tilley lamp and a candle for light. No bathroom; our method of having a bath, which was every Friday night, was in a tin bath. No running water, only a pump at the bottom of our yard. When heavy frost came, this would cause the pipes to freeze, leaving us with no other option but to carry water in buckets from our neighbour's spring well. This happened quite often in the winter. I can recall many a day when the icicles hung from the roof of our house, twelve inches long or more. My

My parents Hugh and May Bradford

father and mother struggled and worked tirelessly each day to bring up their little family and I can honestly say that there was never a day or night passed but my parents saw that their family had enough to eat and drink. Together, with hard work from us all, we managed to get through each day.

In those days nearly every farm had a number of workers or farm hands, especially when the season came round to reap their harvest. This could have been the pulling of their flax, potato gathering or the cutting of hay and barley when the threshing machine, driven by a Fordson tractor, was used. The wee grey 'Fergie' was also very much in use then. Our farm, like many others, was a mixed farm. We kept a few cows which had to be hand milked in the morning and again in the evening. This milk was for our own use and for feeding the little calves. We also made our own homemade butter and most of it was sold to the local shop at Kilkinamurray, just up the road a short distance from where we lived. This wee shop was owned and run by my Aunt Caroline Skelly, my mother's sister.

Hens and bantams were seen running around in the field in front of our house. Their eggs were for our own use and for baking, when the old time griddle was brought out and lovely soda and wheaten farls were made. I loved to watch my mother as she turned them over on the griddle to cook. At night my mother always saw that the hens were closed into a wooden ark as foxes were very numerous then. My mother always had a love for turkeys; she usually had an order of approximately fourteen to sixteen oven ready turkeys each Christmas season and the money would be used to buy the groceries on our Christmas grocery list. My father kept a flock of sheep and took a great interest in protecting them, especially at the so-called 'lambing season' when vulnerable lambs were born. Again, prowling foxes were always in search of prey for food to eat. I can recall on many occasions that it was the custom of my father, before he retired to bed, to go out to the field to attend to his sheep and lambs, as in the winter there was often drifting snow and heavy winds. Even these conditions did not deter him from carrying out his duties.

I never remember my mother driving a car, so on a Friday my father would take her by car to the nearby shop to get some grocery items that the travelling grocery van didn't sell. I really looked forward to this as my mother always brought me two ounces of imperial mint sweets. These had to last me for one week but I was very happy and content.

My mother often reminded me of a serious and almost fateful incident which took place in my young life. In those days we were happy to have the travelling bread van which came and stopped at our door to sell the bread. On this occasion I went with my mother to buy some bread from the 'breadman', as he was called. There was an old well full of water just beside where the van was parked. I got free from my mother's hand and wandered off and fell into the well, down to the bottom. Only for the quick thinking of the breadman who pulled me out of the well and resuscitated me, clearing my airways, I would have died. My mother always reminded me that it was the goodness of an almighty God that my life was preserved at that time.

As time passed and we got older, each one in our family had their own jobs to do on the farm. My father was strict and all orders given were carried out. We were aware of the punishment that we would receive if we disobeyed. The wooden spoon, belt or strap was used then. I was taught from a very early age to respect my parents, my neighbours and friends, both Catholic and Protestant, old and young alike.

Our home was a home where the Bible was brought down from the shelf, opened and read in our midst. Each one of us were taught from God's word how sin entered into the world, (Genesis 2:16,17), and the creation of man and woman and their fall into sin in the Garden of Eden. God commanded them saying, "Of every tree of the garden thou mayest freely eat: but of the tree of the knowledge of good and evil, thou shalt not eat of it: for in the day that thou eatest thereof thou shalt surely die." Satan, the devil, deceived them, intruding into their minds, saying, "Ye shall not surely die." Adam and Eve saw that the tree was good for food and was pleasant to the eyes, so they disobeyed God's righteous demand, took from it and did eat. This was man's fall, the defiance of man against God. This is called sin.

From a very early age I was sent along to Sunday School each Sunday morning. I attended the local Presbyterian Sunday School in the townland of Kilkinamurray. There I was taught from the catechism and from the Scriptures. In the afternoons, during the summer months, I attended another Sunday School in Shanaghan Gospel Hall. This hall was only a short walking distance from our home. There I was taught also from the word of God by faithful Sunday School teachers, such as the late Mr John Hogg, Mr William Redmond, Mr Bobby Adams, Mr Bobby Ringland, Mr David Kernaghan and Miss Hunter. These men and women were all saved and had a desire to teach the children. I was encouraged to learn all the well-known Scriptures, such as John 3:16 and Romans 10:9. Romans 3:22,23 were impressed on my young mind. "For there is no difference: for all have sinned, and come short of the glory of God." When it came to the end of the summer season I was always handed a lovely gift for my attendance, either a Bible or a lovely picture with a verse of Scripture on it. This picture was later seen hanging on the wall in our bedroom - God's word was always in my view to read.

Starting School

Soon it was time to start our local school at Closkelt Primary School. Being the youngest child in the family, my two sisters,

Mary and Jean, had a big responsibility to fulfil, trying to get me to school on time for the start of R.E. (Religious Education) class which was held each morning before school class commenced at 9:15am. I can recall entering the building on my first few mornings at school. I cried and cried because I missed my mother's love and support. As time passed, I soon settled down and made new friends. To my shame I started to say and do things, which if my parents had known, they would have been very displeased.

The headmaster of this school was the late Mr Hayden Warman, formerly from Rosebrook Cottage, Talgarth in Powys, Wales, who lived in Rathfriland. Mr Warman was very strict, especially in timekeeping and homework, and insisted that we speak only when we were spoken to. He always kept a cane beside him as he sat in the armchair at his desk in front of the class. I was a real chatterbox and quite often I was brought up to the front of the class and told to hold out my hand. Once I got a few slaps from the cane I soon sat up and obeyed his instructions. When my mother found out that

School Days: Front L to R - Mary, Myrtle, William
Back - John, Jean

I had to receive the cane for misbehaviour, her reply was, "If you spare the rod, you spoil the child." This was instilled in my young mind.

Harvest Season

I have very clear memories of harvest season, when around July my father made preparation for the hay being cut down, followed by the mowing down of the barley straw.

The tractor and the reaper were brought out of the shed and they both were given a good MOT. My father would open up the field by cutting the grass with a hand scythe around the entrance gate to allow the tractor and hay reaper access to the field, ready for work. This process had to be completed in dry weather, so when the time was right my father would say, "We are ready; all hands on board."

My brother, William, was responsible for driving the tractor, leaving my father to operate the reaper. William, being a fast driver, did not give us much time to gather up the sheaves, to tie them and throw them out of the way. My mother saw that we got our food and I always loved to see her coming through the gate, laden down with a large carrying bag and box of fresh homemade sandwiches. It wasn't long until William stopped the tractor, for he dearly loved his food, especially his mug of tea! It was lovely for us all to be united together with my father and mother as we sat at the bottom of the field enjoying a good old chat and all the good food that my mother had provided. This was an ongoing practice for my mother during the harvest season.

In September and October, when the weather was a lot cooler, it was time to dig the potatoes. In my young days the potatoes had to be gathered in by hand. This was something I did not look forward to, as it was hard work, a rather backbreaking experience. My father always liked a Saturday when all the children were off school. Many of them were seen in our fields, working hard, gathering the potatoes. They enjoyed it and they looked forward to the evening time when my father called it a day, stopping the machinery, then it was time for them to receive their wages. After all, they had worked hard for them, but unfortunately I received nil payment. However, I really enjoyed the company and the good old gossip which was all about school days.

Soon we parted from each other and everyone went their separate ways. When I returned home, feeling very tired, I sat down in the chair and started to ponder over the last few hours. What did this word 'wages' really mean? I soon learned that it was a payment for those who had worked

Dad and brother William making hay

for it. A verse, found in the Scriptures, which was taught in Sunday school, came to me. "For the wages of sin is death; but the gift of God is eternal life through Jesus Christ our Lord" (Romans 6:23). As I was very young at the time I did not really take in the true meaning of this verse.

Coming Home from School

On our way to school we had to pass an old cottage. Its occupant was a dear elderly man. On many occasions on our return home from school we would pay him a visit and he was glad to see us. I always thought he was very lonely and perhaps he was not getting his proper meals. In those days there were no home helps and no 'meals on wheels'. Instead, neighbours and families looked out for each other, irrespective of religion. Everyone was treated equally. This elderly man, named Elias, would have been a distant relative of my father, so he felt a great responsibility towards him and became anxious about his welfare. Consequently, my father offered him a room in our home. He quickly accepted this great offer. Arrangements were made and alterations took place in our house. This meant an extra bedroom had to be found. There were stairs leading up to the old attic, which was very seldom used as it had no insulation; just the bare walls were seen. We could see the slates on the roof and the very atmosphere felt cold. Two double beds were erected for the five of us, and, of course, me being the youngest of the girls, I was stuck in the middle. However, I didn't mind for I got the heat from both my sisters, Mary and Jean. In wintertime it was bitterly cold with heavy frosts and blinding storms of wind and snow. I was always complaining of being cold. Extra blankets were put on our beds. The old crockery bed jar was also filled with hot water and placed in the bottom of the bed to keep our feet warm.

Elias settled well into our home and new surroundings. He loved to go out for short walks up and down the road and my father and mother liked to give him as much independence as possible. One day he decided to walk to the nearby shop to buy tobacco for his pipe. He was well clothed for the wintry conditions. I stood and watched him disappear out of sight. A short time later my father noticed flakes of snow falling and then the wind started to rise. Soon there was a real snow blizzard. My father became deeply concerned about Elias. Where would he be? Would he have reached the shop or was he on his way home? How was he to find out? Telephones were not available in many homes; there were only phone boxes here and there throughout the countryside. But my father didn't give up - his main priority was to go and search for Elias. My eldest brother, William, who had just turned sixteen years of age, went to assist my father. He brought out the wee grey Fergie tractor, hooked on the link box and the two of them went up the road to find this dear man. I was frightened and worried as the winds became stronger and the snow drifts rose. Sadly, they found his body in one of the snow drifts. He had passed away. Sometime later his body was returned to our home. There was deep sadness in our home. I can well remember

Mum and Myrtle standing in front of Dad's Ford Prefect car

neighbours calling to our house but in my young mind I really did not understand much about death. What did it mean? I had not considered that death was a natural occurrence that everyone must face, sooner or later.

A few days after the funeral, the reality of death started to dawn upon me. Elias would not be back. He was gone, never to return. This tragedy was much talked about for some considerable time. Each time I entered his bedroom my eyes seemed to fall on the empty chair where he often sat and those words penetrated my mind - "Gone, no coming back." I do believe that God was speaking to me again through this tragic death. But, as time passed, I returned to school and these thoughts soon left me.

Hallowe'en

I looked forward to Hallowe'en time as my mother always baked a big apple dumpling with custard running down the sides of it. The whole family would gather round the table and my mother saw that we all got our fair share. It went down a treat! Afterwards we had a few games. In one, we had to dip our heads into a dish of water to try and lift, with our teeth, whatever was placed at the bottom. This could have been an apple, a shilling, a sixpence or a three-penny piece. I would try very hard, for whatever you lifted, you got to keep. When this was over and all the water that covered the floor was mopped up, my two brothers, William and John, and I met up with a few friends from school. My brothers were game for anything, so off we set, walking around the countryside, knocking at doors and then running away to hide. We would let down bicycles tyres. Bicycles were very common then because many people couldn't afford a car. We did not realise the hardships we were causing these people. Perhaps their bicycle was their only means of transport to get them to work or to school and they would not have realised there was a problem with the tyres until they set off the following morning. Someone came up with the idea of removing the gates to the fields that ran up the side of the road and hiding them so that the farmers would have to go looking for them. All we were interested in was fun, but I never thought that this was a very dangerous and serious act. There were usually cattle, sheep, horses or cows in the fields, and they were then able to escape out through the now-open gap.

One night after returning home from our wonderful experience, a knock came to our door. My heart started to tremble as I wondered who it could be. Was it a policeman? Had someone seen us do these serious acts with the farmers' gates? Instead, it was one of our neighbours, who had called to inform my father that his cattle were out of the field and were grazing along the side of the road at a bad bend. He was afraid that someone would come around the corner in a car or on a bicycle and there would be "a serious accident and perhaps loss of life." Do you know, I nearly froze in bed as I heard those words?! I can recall that my father was not very pleased. My brothers were called upon to help him as he went to investigate this terrible news. They jumped out of bed and got dressed; everything happened so quickly. Away up the road the three of them went with a torch. Someone had taken off the gate and had set it up against the ditch further down the road. It took some time to get the cattle back into the field with no one getting hurt. As I lay in my bed, I started to think over my last few hours and about the terrible acts that each one of us had been involved in around our area. Were the farmers whose gates we removed experiencing the same heartache as my father? Our silly pranks soon came to an end.

At the age of nine I was well aware that what I had been involved in was totally wrong. I had been breaking one of the Ten Commandments - "Thou shalt not steal" - as recorded in Exodus 20:15. This refers to any act by which a person wrongfully deprives another person of his or her property and it teaches respect for private property. Stealing is an act of sin. What does God's word say about sin, our sin? It separates us from God, as recorded in Romans 3:23. It also controls every area of our lives - what we do, where we go, what we think. God's all-seeing eye is upon each one of us and all our sins are recorded in Heaven.

During my time at school I made many friends. We walked home together and played together, but sadly I can never remember sin and its consequences being considered or talked about. My sister, Jean, was soon to leave school to seek employment so John, Jean, and I decided to mitch school for one day just to be able to tell family and friends of our wonderful experience of dodging school. I can say now that it was an experience I never will forget. In those days a male visitor called into our school to check the pupils' names on the roll book. No one knew when he would appear. We called him the 'Kid Catcher'.

The morning arrived and it was a lovely day, so off we went up the road with our lunches in our schoolbags. When we came to the foot of what was called Burrow's Hill, we watched very carefully to see if anyone was around. One by one we jumped over the hedge into a field which had a large trench at the bottom of it. This was to be our hiding place for the next few hours. How boring it was! It seemed to be a very long day and none of us had the privilege of owning a watch. How were we to know the time? To make matters even worse, John made a comment which alarmed and disturbed me - "What if the Kid Catcher arrives at school today and finds our names omitted on the roll book?" I was frightened. It was not long after this that we decided to watch for an escape route to head for home. When the time was right and all seemed clear, up we got, with our school bags, out of the trench. We jumped over the hedge and walked home as if nothing unusual had happened. When we arrived home, which I believe was an hour and a half early, my mother found it very strange that we were home from school at that hour of the day. We made up a story, a deliberate lie, that the teacher was very generous towards us and let us off school early. We deceived our mother and father, leading them to believe that we were telling the truth.

Visiting Grandpa and Granny Skelly

I loved to go with my mother up to Grandpa and Granny Skelly's house as they also lived on a farm, only on a larger scale than ours. Grandpa kept a large number of sows and little piglets. Some of the sows were cross, and we weren't allowed to go near them. I can remember on one occasion a friend of ours, called Bernard, came from Belfast to visit us and we decided to visit Grandpa's farm. On our arrival, Bernard, coming from a city like Belfast, was overwhelmed by seeing so many sows and piglets on one farm and he opened all the doors of the pig houses and let all the piglets out into the enclosed yard and they all got mixed up. What a mess we got ourselves into! When Grandpa became aware of what had taken place, he was very angry with us. Of course, none of us would own up as to who was to blame. Grandpa sent us home and we were barred from the farm for some time and rightly so. Again I was found in the company of those who set out to cause harm and a measure of frustration both to the piglets and Grandpa. The thought came before me, 'If Grandpa is angry with us, what about God?' We read in Psalm 7:11 that God is angry with the wicked every day and if we do not obey God's word a very sad consequence will come upon us. We will be barred from Heaven, not just for a period of time, but for all eternity. As time passed we were eventually allowed to go back again to the farm, but on one condition, "Do not go near the pig houses."

I dearly loved my Granny Skelly. She was such a lovely, caring lady and talked to me about her Saviour that she trusted so many years ago. I soon learned that Granny was not only saved and on her way to Heaven, but she was also baptised as a believer in the Lord and was in happy fellowship with the believers at Shanaghan Gospel Hall. Granny was a lady who loved to sing hymns and choruses, some I knew and some I didn't. One that I learnt at Sunday school and which she quite often sang was:

> What can wash away my stain?
> Nothing but the blood of Jesus.
> What can make me whole again?
> Nothing but the blood of Jesus.
>
> O, precious is the flow
> That makes me white as snow,
> No other fount I know,
> Nothing but the blood of Jesus.
>
> For my cleansing this I see,
> Nothing but the blood of Jesus.
> For my pardon, this my plea;
> Nothing but the blood of Jesus.
>
> Nothing can for sin atone;
> Nothing but the blood of Jesus.
> Naught of good that I have done;
> Nothing but the blood of Jesus.
>
> This is all my hope and peace;
> Nothing but the blood of Jesus.
> This is all my righteousness;
> Nothing but the blood of Jesus.

Mr Robert Lowry (1826–1899)

I was blessed with a lovely singing voice and very often I would join with her in song. Granny Skelly just loved this.

My father was a keen player of both the mouth organ, and the hand fiddle. Very often, after returning from his outside duties, he would settle into his favourite armchair with his hand fiddle and play some lovely tunes. My sister, Mary, had already taken music lessons with a music teacher and was learning to play the piano. My mother, my sister, Jean, and

I would stand around the piano and join in singing those hymns and choruses we had learnt in Sunday school. I must admit that we, as a family, were all blessed with singing voices.

My mother liked to bake. She often made apple tarts, rhubarb tarts, sponges, pastry, flan cases and scones. Sometimes she needed an item that she had forgotten to get from the shop, so Jean, John and I were sent up to Auntie Caroline's shop to buy it. We began to like the idea of visiting the shop on a regular basis. This shop also had petrol pumps which were installed in view of the shop window. On many occasions when Auntie Caroline was outside to serve petrol we filled our pockets with sweets. Soon we got the item that my mother required and returned home, but with no sweets - we had eaten them all. Again, I deceived Auntie Caroline.

The next time we tried to steal sweets we were caught red-handed. Auntie Caroline told my mother what we had done, that we were stealing her sweets. It had even come to the stage that she hated to see us come through the door. As you can imagine, my mother was very angry and threatened to let my father know that we were again involved in stealing. I knew that God had seen us again and had it recorded in Heaven. This gave my young mind concern. I had told lies, I had stolen and this was sin. I was soon to realise that, if I continued on this path, I would never be in Heaven, but again, being so young, these thoughts soon disappeared out of my mind.

Accident at Home

Time had passed and my eldest brother, William, decided to apply for his driving licence as many of his friends were driving and some had their own motorbikes. He was seventeen years old and in those days a driving test was not enforced.

It wasn't long until his first motorbike was purchased. I often watched him as he sped up the road on it. I became frightened and thought to myself, 'I will certainly not be on that machine with him to risk losing my life.' However, unknown to me, those thoughts were to change.

Just a few weeks before I was due to leave Closkelt Primary School, I was to experience an incident that took place in our home, leaving me with a severe burn on the top of my foot. I was always complaining to my mother about having cold feet due to the heavy frosts and snow and quite often I would pull the chair up to the old black stove, open the oven door, take a seat and stick my feet into it. Oh boy, what heat; it was just amazing!

However, this idea of mine was soon to alter to a different heat as Jean reached over me to lift a kettle of boiling water to make tea for us. Some of the boiling water splashed over the top of my foot, and with the shock of it all, my reaction was swift. I whipped my sock off and with it came the skin on top of my foot. The pain was almost unbearable. Soon I was on my way to the nearby surgery in Ballyward, about three miles from where we lived. Our practitioner then was named Doctor Wilson.

Doctor Wilson, now deceased, lived in a two-storey dwelling and had his own dispensary, where all the medicines and treatments were administered by qualified staff. As I continued to visit the surgery to get my dressings renewed, God spoke to me. The thought came before me, 'If a wee burn on my foot is almost unbearable, what is Hell going to be like?' Again the devil dispersed these thoughts.

It had now come to my last week of school. I was desperate to be with my school friends. My brother saw how anxious I had become, so he offered me his help. He would transport me to school on the back seat of his motorbike and would return for me at 3.00pm. This was another decision I had to make. Will I, or will I not? Dare I risk it; would my life be in danger? My answer was, "Yes," but on one condition, that he drive easy.

Gospel Meetings

In the month of October 1958, two well-known evangelists came to Shanaghan Gospel Hall to commence special gospel meetings. They were the late Mr Thomas Wallace from Ballymena and Mr Robert Beattie from Omagh. The gospel was faithfully preached and souls were awakened as to their need of salvation if ever they intended to be in Heaven. Jean, Mary and I attended these meetings nightly. Two of our friends with whom we sat in the Sunday School got saved. To my surprise the next one to get saved was my sister, Jean.

It was on a Saturday night. My mother was out milking the cows. As Jean sat in the chair, beside the old black stove, she was miserable. The thought came to her mind, 'It's tonight or never.' She knew she was a sinner on the way to a lost eternity, known as Hell. She started to read the Scriptures and these words came before her, "He took the guilty sinner's place and suffered in my stead." Salvation is free. Just there and then she took her place as a sinner. Christ died for sinners, 'therefore, Lord, for me'. Jean was saved in a moment of time, at the age of eighteen years. Here was the first girl in our home to profess faith in Christ. She later received the assurance of salvation when Hebrews 8:12 came to her mind: "For I will be merciful to their unrighteousness, and their sins and their iniquities will I remember no more." She knew it was from the Lord. The news struck my heart like a dagger. I felt really sick and at that time I also had thoughts of getting saved. These meetings soon came to an end, leaving me still to remain in my sins and to continue on in my old sinful nature. I was only fourteen years old, but old enough to read and understand the Scriptures. 1 Peter 5:8

says; "The devil (Satan), as a roaring lion, walketh about, seeking whom he may devour." This was true in my own condition.

William's Wedding

A year or so after William got his motorbike, he purchased his first motorcar and when every opportunity arose he was seen travelling up the road in it. It did not seem to matter how short his journey was, William drove his motorcar. In fact, it had reached the stage that we had nicknamed him 'the traveller'. However, he soon got used to our remarks and saw the funny side to it.

Soon he had a lady sitting in the front seat with him. I was very excited - who could this lady be? I soon learned that her name was Margaret and she lived in Banbridge. Margaret and William started their romance and very soon I was invited as a guest to their wedding.

As this was to be my first invitation to a wedding, it never crossed my mind that marriage was a serious commitment to make to each other. It was, as Scripture tells us in 1 Corinthians 7, the linking of a man and woman together in holy matrimony for a lifetime. This is why male and female need to spend time in each other's company to talk together, to be happy together and to know one another's objectives, priorities and beliefs. They must be physically attracted and need to be together to share their interests on a mental and spiritual plane. This is God's word for a happy and a lasting marriage.

A few months passed and I was invited as a guest to my second wedding. My sister, Jean, was in a happy relationship with a young man named William. William came from Rathfriland, known as 'the town on the top of the hill'. I cannot remember much about the wedding, only that on this occasion I was wearing a brown woolly suit, straight knee length skirt, a woolly hat and brown flat shoes to match. However, I thought I was the most beautiful guest that day; others, I am sure, had other ideas and rightly so!

Chapter 2

Leaving School

Soon I left school and all my companions there, each of us going our separate ways. It was a sad time. There I was, going out into a dark world to seek employment. My first job was in Ferguson's weaving factory on the Lurgan Road, Banbridge, where Jean, my sister, worked. We had little money so we both cycled about seven miles to start work at 8:00am. When 5:00pm came, we cycled back home again. This was an ongoing routine for quite some time.

After a while, I began to be unsettled, being closed in such an environment. I wanted to work in a place more open to the public. I left my employment with Ferguson's Factory and started to work in Wellworth's in Newry Street, Banbridge, (where Supervalu is at this present time) as a shop assistant. Now, this was work that I did really enjoy, for it gave me an insight into how to address the public and to deal with their requests. Jean was soon to seek new employment as well. Her ambition was to become a qualified hairdresser.

The year of 1960 was a year that I will always remember. One day, during the summer, I decided to go for a ride on my bicycle around the countryside. While cycling, I met one of my school friends, and we had a little chat about our school days, both the good times and the bad times. We laughed and joked a lot. Then to my surprise she told me that she had been attending gospel meetings held in a tent, conducted by the Faith Mission pilgrims. This tent was pitched on a site not far from where she lived and she had got saved.

This came as a great shock to me. Not because she had got saved, but because she was a girl who had not had the privilege I had of being brought up in a Christian home. She was now on her way to Heaven, and there I was, still in my sins. I started to attend those meetings and became concerned about my own salvation. One night on returning home after the meeting, I remember thinking, 'I will have to face eternity sometime.' All I wanted at that time was to obtain salvation and to be sure of Heaven. I opened my Bible at John 6:37. I looked at it and read it. "Him that cometh to me I will in no wise cast out." The thought came before me, 'I believe what this verse says, therefore I'm saved.' The devil used his power to convince me that this was God's way of salvation. I felt I must tell my parents, for they had both prayed earnestly for my salvation. They were overjoyed to hear their youngest girl tell them that she had got saved.

Once again I had a desire to leave my employment, this time to take up a nursing career. I began as an assistant nurse, caring for the elderly in the Cowan Heron Hospital in Dromore. The matron at the hospital was called Miss Wallace, a lovely lady. When I went for my first interview with Miss Wallace she informed me that there were special rules which had to be kept. We were to arrive in

The commencement of my nurse training taken in the grounds of Cowan Heron Hospital, Dromore, 1962

time for duty, our appearance had to be neat and tidy, and long hair had to be tied back. A ward note would be made out and put up on the notice board in her office. On Sunday I would be required to work from 8:00am until 2:00pm or 2:00pm until 8:00pm. She also told me of strict rules which were the hospital's policies. One was that if I intended to leave the hospital after coming off duty at 8:00pm I had to report to her first and return to be in bed for 10:00pm. I thought to myself, 'She is not going to give me much leeway here,' but if I wanted to be a successful student, I must abide by the rules. Here I was to leave the comforts of a godly home, my mother, father, brothers and sisters and take my journey out into a cold, evil world where sin was abounding all around us. Many people had no time for the gospel or even to read the Bible.

As I settled into my accommodation in the hospital and commenced my nursing duties, I was introduced to a staff nurse known as Miss Sally Adair. Sally was a true friend to me. She was like the hen, and me, her chick. Sally became like a second mother to me. She was saved and on her way to Heaven and often spoke to me about her Saviour. She was my shelter. After a few weeks on duty, death became a reality to me as, for the first time, I watched a patient taking their last breath; a permanent end of life, a soul going from time into eternity. My heart was deeply touched as the thought came before me, 'Eternity where?'

As time passed, death just became to me as the end of life down here on earth. On my days off duty I would take a walk down into Dromore Square to stroll around the shops and perhaps buy an ice-cream out of Jackie Reid's ice-cream parlour. It went down a treat.

There was a dear man who visited our home regularly. His name was Mr Alfie Beggs and he lived in Meeting Street in the town. He had two daughters, named Elizabeth and Sally, who still lived with him. I got to know them and quite often I was found in their company and made many new friends, most of whom were Christians. One young man I met was named Martin Beggs. We got into a great conversation about our jobs, what he did and what I was interested in. Then we talked about spiritual matters. I told Martin I was saved and that both my parents were saved long before I was born. I soon learned that Martin was saved on the night of the 1st October 1960 after coming home from a gospel meeting conducted by two well-known evangelists, the late Mr Eddie Fairfield and the late Mr William Bunting. Martin got saved in his own bedroom. Later he told me he was baptised and was in happy fellowship with the assembly gathering in the Gospel Hall, Gallows Street, Dromore.

When I was off duty on a Sunday morning I began to attend the remembrance meeting, which was held in the Gospel Hall in Gallows Street at 11:00am. I remember the first time that I was present to witness and observe the Christians – those who were saved and baptised – sitting around the Lord's table to remember the Lord. I sat in the back seat and listened, as they sang hymns and prayed, giving God thanks for His Son. Their thoughts were centred on the crucifixion of our blessed Saviour, Jesus Christ, His trials, death, burial, resurrection and His ascension to glory.

The Scriptures which were brought before us were found in Luke's gospel - Christ's death

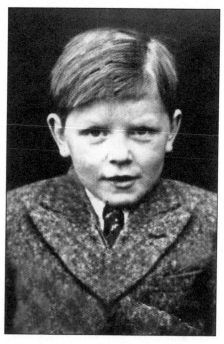

My husband Martin in School days

34

in chapter 23, and His resurrection in chapter 24. I was deeply touched and impressed, as there was a sense of God's presence in their midst and peace and calmness were seen in their very countenances. Then another man would stand up and give out a hymn from the Believers Hymn Book. One hymn that was given out and sung beautifully was:

Abba, Father! We approach Thee
In our Saviour's precious name;
We, Thy children, here assembling,
Access to Thy presence claim;
From our sin His blood hath washed us;
'Tis through Him our souls draw near,
And Thy Spirit, too, hath taught us,
Abba, Father! name so dear.

Once as prodigals we wandered
In our folly, far from Thee;
But Thy grace, o'er sin abounding,
Rescued us from misery:
Thou Thy prodigals hast pardoned,
Loved us with a Father's love;
Welcomed us with joy o'erflowing,
E'en to dwell with Thee above.

Clothed in garments of salvation,
At Thy table is our place;
We rejoice, and Thou rejoicest,
In the riches of Thy grace:
It is meet, we hear Thee saying,
We should merry be and glad;
I have found My once lost children,
Now they live who once were dead.

Abba, Father! all adore Thee,
All rejoice in Heaven above;
While in us thy learn the wonders
Of Thy wisdom, power and love;

Soon, before Thy throne assembled,
All Thy children shall proclaim,
Glory, everlasting glory,
Be to God and to the Lamb.

James G Deck

As I sat there and joined in with the singing, I thought, 'What a gathering!' There was something real about this company. One of the men gave thanks for the bread, which speaks of the sufferings of our blessed Lord Jesus Christ for our sins, after which it was passed around for those in fellowship to partake of. Another man then gave thanks for the wine, which speaks of His precious blood that was shed. This also was passed around. Before the remembrance meeting came to an end, the Scriptures were again opened and read. Good ministry was given to all present. After the closing prayer, I had to return to the hospital to be ready for duty at 2:00pm. The following week I was found at the Sunday night gospel meeting, which commenced at 6:00pm and lasted for one hour.

I still had an eye for Martin, as we spoke quite often to each other. We began our romance and little did I realize that Martin was to ask my father if he would have any objections to us getting married. Some three years later I finished my nurse training. Very soon I was introduced to Martin's parents, Walter and Elizabeth Beggs. They

Martin's parents
Walter & Elizabeth Beggs 1956

also lived in Meeting Street. I found them both pleasant and easy to communicate with. They gave me a great welcome into their home and it wasn't long until my feet were found under the table, eating my dinner with the rest of the family. Sometime later, after reading the Scriptures on believer's baptism, a verse came to my mind. "He that believeth and is baptized shall be saved" (Mark 16:16). It suddenly came to me like this: believing comes first, then baptism, but this time by immersion, or submerging, under the water. I approached the overseers and told them of my concern, of how I would like to be baptised and obey God's command. I gave them an outline of my experience and profession. It was on my own confession of faith I was baptised in Banbridge Gospel Hall, Banbridge, by the late Mr Samuel Foster from Loughbrickland. Later I was received into fellowship in the assembly in Dromore.

Myrtle receiving final certificate in nursing 1956

As I continued my nursing studies, I had to move to new lodgings because my next employment was in the Lagan Valley Hospital, Lisburn. I was sorry to leave Dromore and my many friends that I had come to know and love. One person who was dear to my heart was Martin. With his love and my love together, our romance began to flourish. Martin gave me great advice from the Scriptures and he sought to help me with all my spiritual needs. We soon got engaged and arrangements were now underway for our wedding day.

Paddle in Newcastle

It was now summertime in the year of 1964. One thing which I looked forward to was getting a weekend off duty. This meant I could return home to my parents to get filled in with all the gossip.

It was a lovely Saturday morning; warm and sunny weather was forecast. Martin suggested taking me to my home farm as my father and the rest of my family were busy in the fields, cutting hay and gathering up the sheaves, ready to make haystacks, as they were called.

When we arrived, Martin and I joined in, helping them as best we could. I enjoyed the day being with my family again, but most of all I had the company of Martin, who would be my husband in a few months' time, God willing.

When the time came to stop work everyone left the field very tired as the heat was almost unbearable. My brother, William, made a surprise proposal to Martin and me - "What about us going up to Newcastle for a paddle or a dip in the sea?" I hesitated for a few minutes and eventually both Martin and I agreed, as we thought it was a wonderful idea. At this stage none of us could swim.

William came up with a great idea to take with us a car

tyre tube and a foot pump to pump it up with. This would give us a measure of security, a life line. When we arrived in Newcastle we found the beach and promenade was packed with people. However, this did not deter us from fulfilling our plans. We travelled on up to the top of the seaside resort and parked our car not far from the Slieve Donard Hotel. From there we carried all our swim gear to a place then called 'the sandbanks'. This was a place where few people were seen. I thought, 'Great, we have the sea to ourselves, no one to bother us!' My brother had already the tube pumped up, ready for use.

Martin was the first to use the tube which was secured around his waist, so on and on we all waded, further and further into the sea, enjoying the waves. None of us realised that the tide was coming in and not going out. It seemed to me that we were in the sea quite some time now and we all thought it was time to return to shore, as we were all feeling very tired and hungry. As we started to wade our way back to the shore, unknown to us, there was a large hollow in the sand. I was terrified as the waves got bigger and stronger. Suddenly, I noticed Martin being turned upside down, the tube came off over his feet and he went down under the water. I started to panic and can remember thinking that we were all going to be overcome with the deep waves. Death was looking me in the face. I was just about to go under the water when William, who was much taller than us, was able to grab the tube and help Martin and me to safety. We were all left in a state of shock. I cannot even remember coming home in the car that night.

As I lay in my bed that night I could not sleep. Many things filled my mind; that which we thought we were enjoying could have led to the loss of our three lives. We had had the sea to ourselves; there had been no one around who could have saved us. The headlines in the newspapers on the Monday morning could have been, "Three lost at sea." Those words echoed through my head. But I am very thankful there was One who had His all-seeing eye upon us, even though I wasn't saved. Underneath and all around us are His everlasting arms. "When thou passest through the waters, I will be with thee" (Isaiah 43:2). This was very true in our case. We were truly 'preserved by Jesus' when we were in danger.

I was now ready to sit my final examination, so we set our wedding date for the 10th March 1965.

The Big Snowfall

1965 was recorded as the 'year of the big snow'. Snow drifts blocked some roads leaving many trapped in their homes. A few weeks before our big day we had received quite a lot of wedding presents, some from my nursing colleagues in the hospital. These had to be delivered to my home at Manse Road, Shanaghan, Katesbridge, as the usual tradition was to allow friends and family to view them and to celebrate such an event over a cup of tea and pastry with my parents.

Martin and I decided to take a chance and deliver our presents to my mother and father's home, so we loaded the presents into Martin's motorcar. People said we were both mad going out in such treacherous conditions, but we thought differently. Off we went through the snow. We eventually got as far as Katesbridge village, about one mile from home, when suddenly we hit a large snow drift which caused the car to stop. By this time the winds were rising and it was snowing quite heavily.

We started to panic. It was only now that we realised that what the people had said to us, that we were both mad, was actually true. However, God was good to us. Nearby a row of terraced houses and I was fortunate to know one of the residents that lived there. He was called Mr Robert Dalzell and he was a man whom I held in high esteem.

Robert was a true gentleman who preached the glorious

message of the gospel. He was also a Sunday School teacher in Shanaghan Gospel Hall, so for many years I had been found in his presence. What were we to do? We had no other option but to arrive at his door to explain to him our dilemma. Robert kindly assisted us by allowing us a space in his home for our wedding presents. Our car was now abandoned, and we both struggled hard through the snow, walking and falling, until we reached my family home.

When my father and mother saw us they too were deeply shocked at our venture. Martin was to spend his first night in our home. What an experience for us both, but especially Martin, spending his first night with his intended in-laws. I often wondered what was going through his mind. Anyhow, morning arrived and the snowploughs started to clear the roads to make a path for the farmers to use their tractors to go to feed their stock in the snow-covered fields.

The snow was slow to melt. We eventually retrieved our motorcar some days later and were able to finally fulfil our plans. Our wedding presents were safely transported to my home in Manse Road.

Chapter 3

Our Wedding

We were married in Banbridge Gospel Hall by the late Mr Jim Hutchinson, a well-known evangelist from Dundonald, but who had been born and brought up in Banbridge.

Martin and Myrtle cutting wedding cake

It was a Wednesday morning and I remember gazing out through the window at the beautiful scene of snow that covered the ground. Soon the sun began to shine. At midday I was on my way to get married to Martin, sitting in the back of the taxi with my father. I felt very proud and happy walking down the aisle, arm in arm with my father who was to give me away in wedlock. After we took our solemn vows, saying, "I do," Martin and I were pronounced husband and wife. Matthew 19:5,6 were quoted, "For this cause shall a man leave father and mother, and shall cleave to his wife: and they twain shall be one flesh...What therefore God hath joined together, let not man put asunder."

As we made our first appearance before a crowd of onlookers, three men came up to us and whipped Martin away from my side. Suddenly, I looked to my right and all I could see was a tractor and trailer which had a bale of hay on it. I was totally shocked, for everything happened so quickly. His colleagues, with whom he had worked in the joinery trade, had decided to give him a surprise send-off. They took him for a trip around Banbridge in the open trailer. Soon Martin returned unharmed and we were on our way to the Savoy Hotel in Portadown for our wedding reception. Our honeymoon was spent in the south of Ireland. We travelled in Martin's old A40 Devon car, a car in which he took great delight - it was always spotless. We had in our possession a sum of forty pounds to pay for lodgings and our meals. After five days we returned home with twelve pounds in our pockets.

Our First Home

We settled into our first home as Mr and Mrs Beggs in a little cottage on the Ballymacormick Road, Dromore. Our weekly rent was twenty-one shillings, and twelve pounds were spent on a second-hand gas cooker from the late Mr Tommy Martin, who owned a shop in the town. Martin was employed with the shipyard in Belfast and I continued to work at the Lagan Valley Hospital in Lisburn.

One night I was coming home after night duty and as I approached the turnoff for Dromore from the dual carriageway, I noticed an accident had taken place. I pulled over onto the hard shoulder, and rushed to the scene. Two cars had crashed into each other, leaving one man injured and another man fighting for his life. I did all I could to try and save his life, but he died. This left a great impact on my mind and I was distressed.

A few months after this accident, I was just getting over the shock of it when Martin, my sister, Jean, and brother-in-law, William, and I were travelling by car to go to Ballynahinch for a meal in a lovely café, known then as Dickson's Restaurant. It was a Saturday evening and on our way we came across another accident involving two cars. We stopped and I jumped out of our car to give my assistance. I found two men trapped in their vehicles. One man I knew – it was Mr Tommy Martin, the man we bought our first cooker from. I stayed with Tommy until the fire brigade and lifting equipment arrived to release him from the wreckage. When the ambulance arrived I accompanied him down to the Lagan Valley Hospital in Lisburn. On our way down the road Tommy and I had a conversation together. Little did I realise these were to be the last words I would speak to him. News came on Monday that Tommy Martin had passed away suddenly in hospital, two days after this terrible accident. Once again I was left devastated.

The Birth of Our First Little Girl

I was now expecting our first child, and on the 12th May 1966 a little baby girl was born. We called her Pamela, and I gave up my work to care for our little baby. I soon got used to the sleepless nights and a baby crying, especially when she was hungry and needed fed. One night Martin and I retired to bed after our little baby was put down to sleep in her cot. Everything was quiet for some time. In the distance I could hear a rumble of thunder and then came the lightning, which lit up the whole bedroom. This was something that I was terrified of - thunder and lightning. Soon the baby started to cry and became very unsettled. As I got up out of bed to try and comfort her, a loud bang and the smashing of glass was heard and then the lights went out. I was frightened. Soon we got the baby settled and as daylight broke we could see the damage that was done in our home. The lightning had travelled up our electric cable, which was attached to a plug in our working kitchen, leading to one of our pig houses which contained a litter of pigs. A large hole was left in the kitchen wall and the lightning bolt had stripped the walls right through the living room. The meter board, which was above the door in the front hall, also was smashed. Martin and I were devastated to see such a mess.

I started to ask myself the question: Why has the Lord allowed this to happen to us? Suddenly the thought struck my conscience - it would be good to go around my own foundation. This stayed with me for some time. What sort of a foundation am I building upon to get me to Heaven? Is it solid or is it like the sand? The devil tried to steer my conscience away from such thoughts. But these thoughts were to stay with me for days. My baby was taking up much of my time and I wasn't at the meetings as often. In my own mind I didn't have the same interest but I put it down to motherhood.

Special Gospel Meetings Commenced

In the month of November 1966, it was announced that special gospel meetings were to commence in a tent beside the old railway station in Dromore. The speaker responsible was Mr Jim Martin, an evangelist from Ballymena. Jim was a genuine Christian preacher of the gospel. He was not interested in people's money, riches or religion. He was a man who obeyed God's word and had a love for everyone. It says in Mark 16:15, "Go ye into all the world, and preach the gospel to every creature." This was Jim's greatest desire

- to reach out to a world where Christ has been rejected by so many.

Jim's preaching was to the point. It was 'turn or burn'. It is Heaven or Hell for all eternity. Once you go over the boundary line into your destination, there is no coming back. Luke 16:26 says "And beside all this, between us and you there is a great gulf fixed", meaning 'fixed permanently'. The devil may give you a sense of self-esteem, or give you a respectable religion, or good works, so that you may think, 'If I do my bit, surely God will do the rest'. Jim would gaze down at his audience and his words were, "Are you saved? I'm not asking you if you have signed a card or put up your hand after an appeal. Maybe you are only depending on a verse of Scripture. I say to you kindly, go around your own foundation. What are you depending on to take you into God's Kingdom?" This was a good question for us and one that never left me.

I returned home very disturbed. God was speaking to me. I started to go around my own foundation. I came to the conclusion that I had only a false profession. I made known to Martin my doubts of salvation. Martin made a great statement - "Myrtle, it is better to find out in time. If you hold on to something that is false, your foundation will crumble down and your soul will be lost forever. Remember, Myrtle, you've got to realise you are a lost sinner and there is nothing you can do to save yourself."

Martin retired to bed. It was on the 21st November 1966 that I made up my mind, "If I'm going to get this great matter of this 'so great salvation' settled, it must be tonight." I read well-known verses from the Bible that I had learnt at Sunday school and gospel tracts that were in a box sitting in the kitchen. I tried to believe, tried to trust, but with all this I was still in the dark and confused.

At last I cried within myself, "Lord, I'm lost and I'm on my way to a lost eternity." It was now 1:05am. I was about to give the whole thing up, as I thought there was no salvation for me. But just in a moment I forgot about my believing and trying to trust. I looked by faith to Calvary's cross and took it in for the very first time, at the age of twenty-one years, that Christ died for sinners. I'm a sinner, so He must have died for me. He became my substitute, therefore I go free. I accepted Christ as my Saviour.

> Because the sinless Saviour died,
> My sinful soul is counted free,
> For God the just is satisfied
> To look on Him and pardon me.

However, before I would say a word to anyone, I needed assurance. I prayed that God would give me Scripture to reassure me that I was truly saved and born again. Just then, a verse of a hymn that was often sung at our gospel meetings came to mind.

> There is life for a look at the crucified One,
> There is life at this moment for thee;
> Then look, sinner, look unto Him, and be saved–
> Unto Him Who was nailed to the tree.

> Then doubt not thy welcome since God hath declared
> There remaineth no more to be done;
> That once, in the end of the world, He appeared
> And completed the work He begun.

> Look! Look! Look and live!
> There is life for a look at the crucified One,
> There is life at this moment for thee.

> Amelia Hull (19th Century)

I made it known to the brethren in Dromore assembly what had taken place in my life and withdrew from the Lord's table on Sunday morning, after reading 1 Corinthians 11:26 regarding partaking of the bread and wine. Verse 27 says,

"Whosoever shall eat of the bread, and drink this cup of the Lord, unworthily, shall be guilty of the body and blood of the Lord." Verse 29 – "For he that eateth and drinketh unworthily, eateth and drinketh damnation to himself, not discerning the Lord's body." I realised now that I had been doing this for almost four years. I had now defeated that old serpent, the devil. What a great discovery! I was able to sing in truth.

> I once was bound in Satan's chains,
> And blinded by his power,
> But Jesus broke my fetters off -
> O blessed, wondrous hour!
> He told me of His love, and drove
> My unbelief away;
> And now I see His face, and joy
> To bow beneath His sway.
>
> Yes, Jesus did it, did it all;
> He saved a worm like me;
> Nor will He rest till I am blest,
> And His full glory see.
>
> Salvation is my happy song,
> Redemption is my theme;
> I bask beneath His blessed smile,
> And drink at life's full stream;
> And in a little while I go
> To dwell with Him on high,
> When not a cloud shall intercept
> The full tide of my joy!
>
> Albert Midlane (1825 –1909)

Sometime later I asked for baptism. This was carried out - I was baptised as a believer in Christ and was received into Dromore assembly, where I still remain, some forty-nine years later.

John's Wedding

It had got to the stage that I liked the idea of being invited to a wedding, as I would say, 'I always got a good feed.' How long would I have to wait for my next invitation to such an event? My brother, John, was now working with Grahams Construction in Dromore, and was in a relationship with a lady called Florence. Florence lived in Dromore. As I watched this space my thoughts were, 'Another wedding for me'. But no, John and Florence had already made their arrangements and unknown to me their date was set. John always said if he was to get married he would go quietly, no fuss and so this was very true of him.

One afternoon John and Florence arrived home and announced to my father and mother that they were now husband and wife. I was pleased for them both.

Mary's Wedding

I was now expecting our second child. My sister, Mary, was still living at home helping my father and mother on the farm. Mary had a great interest in farming and was now in a steady relationship with a farmer from Donaghmore, Newry, known as Sydney. It came to my attention that Mary and Sydney had set the date to get married and my sister, Jean, and I were asked to be in attendance as matrons of honour at their wedding, which was arranged for November 1967.

My heart started to beat quickly. Oh dear, what was I to do? I was now seven months pregnant with my second child. This was another decision for me. Would I or would I not? I didn't want to let my sister down, nor did I want to make a show piece of myself, Martin or my family. We talked it through and I decided I would be a matron of honour, provided everything was going well.

The next few weeks were a very anxious time for Martin and me, and as time passed my dress had to be altered accordingly until it finally came to the day of the wedding. Although the weather was cold, I really enjoyed the day and was very pleased that I was able to fulfil my sister's request. I can say that God was watching over me.

Our Second Child is Born

A few weeks later, on the 9th January 1968, my second daughter was born, a wee sister for Pamela. We named her Sharon Lenise. It was only when I returned home from hospital with baby Sharon that the realisation of more sleepless nights hit me. Would I be able to cope with my everyday duties, not only the upkeep of cleaning my home, but the changing of nappies and feeding my two little girls? Would I be a good mother to them both?

Sharon was a very contented little baby. Once she was given her bottle and got her nappy changed, she went back to sleep. Soon she was sleeping throughout the night. To my surprise, Sharon started to walk at a very early age. This meant that I was under quite a lot of pressure as Sharon was able to walk to the cupboards, open the doors and pull everything out. It did not matter what it was - saucepans, tea towels, cooking utensils - all landed on the floor!

Both Pamela and Sharon would argue over the toys that covered the living room floor. Sometimes I felt like blowing a fuse or blowing my top! One thing Martin and I were concerned about was the lack of space. After much consideration we bought a house on the Gowdystown Road, about five miles from the town of Banbridge.

The Richardsons

In 1969 my father's cousin, Mrs Minnie Richards from

Canada, was to visit my mother and father's home in Northern Ireland, accompanied by her son, John, and his wife, Norma, and two little girls, Joy and Trudy.

As they arrived at our home in Manse Road and took up residence for a few weeks they became interested in their family tree. I thought how amazing Minnie was for her years. She was a lovely lady. We spent many happy hours together going through old photographs. They spent many days visiting friends and collecting information.

A few days before they were due to leave for home, my mother was tipped off about a special birthday. Trudy, one of the little girls, was to celebrate her fifth birthday. My mother baked a special cake and we all had a great party. The children and I enjoyed every minute of it. It was a

The Bradford family with the Richardson family from Canada. The tallest man at back row is John Richardson below John, his wife Norma, also their two girls in checked dresses, Joy and Trudy, Minnie my dad's cousin last lady on right, left side Alfred Beggs with glasses, Martin's uncle

time to remember. I was really sad when we had to say our goodbyes.

Sadly, this was the last time for Minnie to visit us as she passed away from time into eternity sometime later.

Chapter 4

My Father's Death

In the year 1970, death was to claim my father. He had been diagnosed three years previously with throat cancer. In those days treatments were not as advanced as they are today. I saw him losing weight and his condition deteriorating, but this did not deter him from working around the farm.

The Bradford family - Front: Mary, Myrtle, Mum, Jean
Back: William, Dad, John

It was a Saturday afternoon. We didn't normally go to the farm at weekends as our girls were very young - Pamela was four years old and Sharon was two years old, but later we could see God's hand in our plans for us to visit my father that afternoon.

When we arrived, we spent some time in the home together in relaxed and informal conversation with both of my parents. My father told us that he had been in the field just across the road from the dwelling house. A lot of water had gathered in the ditch, so his method was to dig in the ditch with the shovel to try to release it. I accompanied him outside and I stood and watched him cross the road and go up the field. Then I returned into the house to be with my mother and my children.

Martin decided to go to the field to investigate what my father was doing and to see if he could give him some assistance. As Martin approached him, he noticed that my father went to reach for the shovel but suddenly collapsed and fell. Initially, Martin thought that he had slipped on the watery surface, but then realised it was more serious than only a loss of balance. Martin pulled him out of the trench and left him down on the grass. At this moment, a local farmer, known as Mr Robert Kernaghan, was passing our home on the tractor. Robert saw the commotion up in the field and he stopped and ran up to Martin.

My brother, William, soon came on the scene to give his assistance, but it was all over for my father, who had passed from time into eternity. Wasn't it good that at the age of thirty years my father trusted Christ as his own and personal Saviour? He could have left the matter of God's great salvation too late. This is why we read in 2 Corinthians 6:2, "Behold, now is the accepted time; behold, now is the day of salvation." Now is the time to get saved, when you are healthy and well. Tomorrow could be too late. The hymnwriter penned these words:

O come, sinner, come,
O, why do you delay?
The pressing invitation is
That you should come today.
Tomorrow has no promise
That it can give to you.
Tomorrow is eternity
Just hidden from your view.

A.N. Curtis (Arr.)

The news soon spread around the district of the sudden death of my dear father. He was seventy years old and had been married for thirty-five years. The funeral was arranged. It was conducted by the late Mr John Hogg from Banbridge and Mr Stanley Wells from Lisburn. All that gathered around to pay their last respects to my father were warned of the brevity - shortness - of a life. Psalm 90:10 was very true regarding my father – "The days of our years are threescore years and ten; and if by reason of strength they be fourscore years, yet is their strength labour and sorrow; for it is soon cut off, and we fly away." As soon as the pulse beat has stopped, another person becomes the 'missing face'.

Expecting our Third Child

I was now expecting our third child. We had already booked a holiday to Douglas on the Isle of Man for one week in the summer of 1970. I had mixed feelings as I was heartbroken but the family encouraged us to go for the break. Martin, our two girls, Pamela and Sharon, and I set off for our first holiday. The plane journey was brilliant and when we arrived in Douglas the sun was shining and it was very hot. We soon settled into our accommodation.

A few days after exploring around Douglas, we eventually came to a place called Summerland. This was a brilliant area for children to play and it was all under one roof. Our children spent some hours there and were sad to leave such a place.

When we returned home, we heard on the radio that a fire had broken out in Summerland in Douglas, Isle of Man. Some had lost their lives and many had suffered severe burns to their bodies. This brought terror to both Martin and I as we thought of the times our own children had enjoyed playing there. It was such a tragedy. Truly God was gracious to us all to allow us to return home safely.

Things were to change in the family home. My father's chair was empty, leaving my mother very lonely. Many ups and downs were to follow, as in every home after losing a loved one. I loved my mother dearly and I sought to give her support when needed. She had just reached the age of sixty-six years. She was always in my thoughts and prayers and I knew that her faith in Christ would bring her through all the heartaches and loneliness that she would experience.

On the 29th January 1971, our third child, Amanda, was born. As our family grew up we realised we needed an extra bedroom. We sold our house, which had only two bedrooms, and bought a building site at Ashfield crossroads. This site was not far up the road from where we were living.

Martin was now working in the building trade with my brother, William, and Mr John McKinley from Dromore. They were all self-employed and built many haysheds, milking parlours, slurry tanks etc. throughout the countryside. Their good workmanship was seen on many farms.

Plans had been accepted for us to build a four bedroom bungalow. Soon the foundations were made ready and the work began. We worked hard to get our bungalow built and to our surprise we had our first Christmas dinner sitting around the table with our little family. This was in the year 1972. We had now settled into our new home.

It was shortly after, that news came that we were having a family member coming to Northern Ireland from the United States of America for approximately ten days who would like to spend time with the Beggs family in Dromore. Soon I learned that it was the Rev. Walter Clarke, his wife, Diane, son, Russell and daughter, Heather. They were friends of my in-laws and this was to be their first visit to Northern Ireland. The family was taking part in a five week Methodist exchange programme in England and they had decided to visit Dromore. This was the town from where Walter's grandfather, Mr Samuel Clarke, had emigrated to America in the year 1923.

Before leaving for America, Samuel, his wife, Anna, and their four children, Jack, Bill, Walter and Evelyn lived at Barban Hill in the town of Dromore. Samuel was a plasterer by trade and had worked on both First Dromore Presbyterian Church and the Banbridge Road Presbyterian Church in Dromore.

Martin and I had the pleasure of having Walter and Diane as our guests while Russell and Heather stayed with other family members. During their visit to Dromore the Clarke family visited extensively with many of their relatives. The Rev. Walter Clarke had the great joy of preaching at morning worship in Banbridge Methodist Church. During their time here they made many friends and we all enjoyed the chat. When it came to the time of their departure many tears were shed as we said our emotional goodbyes. We felt the parting of the Clarke family very deeply and this feeling continued for some time.

Near to our bungalow, on the other side of Ashfield crossroads, there was a wooden building situated in the corner of a field where children's meetings were held each Monday night in the autumn season. This work was organised by two local brethren. One was the late Mr Robert Graham from Dromore Gospel Hall and the other was the late Mr Tommy Alderdice from Mullafernaghan Gospel Hall. These two men had something in common - they were both saved and on their way to Heaven and their desire was to teach the young children from the word of God. There is nothing else but the word of God to bring conviction to the heart and salvation to the soul. One never should be ashamed to use it or read it to the children. Psalm 119:130 says, "The entrance of thy words giveth light", so why try to bring light by using anything else? Romans 10:17 says, "So then faith cometh by hearing, and hearing by the word of God." We must get the Scriptures firmly implanted into the hearts and minds of our young people. I can say that the teaching of the two Christian gentlemen was centred only on the Scriptures. These included Bible lessons, memory verses, quizzes and choruses. We saw that our children were sent along each Monday night and it thrilled my heart to hear them say the verses they had learned from the Scriptures and to sing all those lovely choruses such as:

> Children, can you tell me why
> Jesus came to bleed and die?
> He was happy, high above,
> Dwelling in His Father's love;
> Yet He left His joy and bliss
> For a wicked world like this.

> Children, I will tell you why
> Jesus left His home on high;
> We were all by sin undone,
> Yet He loved us every one:
> So to earth He kindly came,
> On the cross to bear our shame.

> He who for our sins was slain
> Lives and dwells above again,
> Where He's waiting to receive
> All who will His love believe.
> This, dear children - this is why
> Jesus came to bleed and die.

One night, coming home from the children's meeting,

Pamela, who was only nine years of age, informed us she had got saved. There was much rejoicing in our home at that time. There is nothing more that thrills the heart of a mother and father than to hear of a member of the family trusting Christ for their salvation and to know that their sins are all taken away. Our prayers were answered.

Australian Visitors

Martin had several cousins living in Australia whom he had never met, although he always had the desire to fulfil his aspiration to visit them. One cousin, who was a frequent visitor to Northern Ireland, was Mr Jim Beggs and his lovely wife, Tui. Jim's father and Martin's father were brothers who were brought up in the townland of Quilly, Dromore.

Jim and Tui were very interested in their family history, or, as we would say, their family tree. Many days were spent going round the churches, visiting the homestead and the farm, which was down a long lane. Graveyards and even headstones were also very much in their itinerary. I was deeply touched at the eagerness of both Jim and Tui and their interest in such a place as Northern Ireland.

On a warm, sunny day there was nothing more pleasing to them than to travel around the Antrim Coast. Martin and I would take them by car, stopping off at different locations to visit the shops. They would buy souvenirs for family and friends back home in Australia. They loved to barbecue and Martin would bring a disposable barbecue with us, plus all the food. It was lovely just to stop at the picnic areas and sit around the table listening to Jim and Tui tell us some of their experiences of life back home in Australia. Some were very emotional stories, and others were about the good times they had enjoyed with their families. Eventually, we travelled on to Portstewart and then Portrush. Both thought these two seaside places were fabulous.

They always wanted to see Newcastle. When the weather was good we set off to visit the Mourne Mountains, stopping off at Legananny Dolmen. Jim and Tui would get out of the car and gaze all around at the superb scenery. It stretched for miles and miles. Jim would stand in amazement and say, "It's wonderful, it's outstanding." Tui was overawed with the beautiful country that we lived in.

Our journey then continued to the favourite seaside resort of Newcastle. This is where the Mountains of Mourne sweep down to the lovely blue sea. Many people, old and young, were seen in the sea. Some were bathing and others were paddling about in their bare feet. Crowds of people were seen lying on the grass on the promenade. Many were enjoying their ice-creams bought at the Strand ice-cream shop just a few yards away.

Newcastle was booming then. Many Sunday School pupils and their parents travelled by bus to this favourite seaside resort to spend the day. This was their annual outing. Many people were seen sitting on the low wall, which stretched for some length up the main street, enjoying the fresh air and the gentle breeze coming from the sea. We sat on the summer seat watching the young boys and girls with their parents, playing down on the sand. Some had their buckets and spades and were making sandcastles, others were playing rounders and many just sat on their rugs and watched.

Jim and Tui had an ear for the gospel and would listen to the open air gospel meetings held on the promenade. First it was the Faith Mission Pilgrims, followed by the brethren from the local Gospel Halls. I can say now, after listening to such messages from the lips of these men, no-one within their hearing was left without excuse as to their eternal destination.

Soon it was time for Jim and Tui to take their flight back home to Australia. Their minds were set on the hope that

Martin, the girls and I would pay them a visit and meet some more of his cousins. Time passed so quickly and, sad to say, we never made the trip over to Australia.

Gospel Meetings, Gowdystown Road

In August 1980, special gospel meetings commenced in a tent, which was erected in a field at Gowdystown Road, Banbridge, near the dual carriageway. The speakers responsible were the late Mr Jim Hutchinson and Mr Jim Allen. We attended these gospel meetings and our second daughter, Sharon, who was only twelve years old, made it known to us that she had got saved on the 15th August, around 8:45pm. She had been listening to Mr Jim Allen, who had read from John 3:16 - "For God so loved the world, that he gave his only begotten Son, that whosoever believeth in him should not perish, but have everlasting life" – and she accepted Christ as her Saviour. Again we were overjoyed, hearing of Sharon getting saved.

Our Fourth Child is Born

On the 4th November 1982, our fourth little girl was born in the maternity ward of the Lagan Valley Hospital, Lisburn. Martin and I decided to call her Martine, after Martin. Martine was born eight weeks premature and because of this she had to be transferred to the Intensive Care Unit at the Royal Victoria Hospital, Belfast where she remained for several weeks.

When we eventually got our little girl home she required many follow-up appointments at a number of hospitals. Transporting my little child to and from hospital for special treatment took up much of my time. However, I did not mind, as Martine was my first priority. This continued on for a period of time.

Daughters: Pamela, Sharon and Amanda

Daughter Martine's first birthday

In July 1986, my father-in-law, Mr Walter Beggs, was taken into Musgrave Park Hospital, Belfast to have surgery for a hip replacement. Walter had his operation and all went well. The day after the surgery, 13th July 1986, he suddenly went into cardiac arrest. The usual procedures were carried out, but even with a team of doctors, he did not survive. Walter had left this scene of time and gone into eternity. He was only sixty-seven years old. Martin and I were deeply shocked to hear the unexpected news, but we had one consolation - he was at home with the Lord. His funeral service was taken by Mr Jack Lennox (evangelist) from Magherafelt. This again left a great void in the Beggs' household.

Once again we had our second holiday booked, this time to go to Blackpool in August for one week. Again the question came to my mind, 'What should we do? Should we go or stay at home?' Our four girls had talked so much about this holiday, seeing Blackpool tower, double decker buses, the trams travelling up and down in the open streets and the piers lit up at night. We decided to go, again with mixed feelings.

We found it a very busy seaside resort and the weather was extremely hot. Every street was buzzing with people, both young and old. The children enjoyed themselves. However, Martin and I were glad to get home safe and well.

Portable Hall Erected in Our Yard

It was a sunny day as I stood in our living room and gazed out through the window. I noticed a car drive into our yard and two men got out and looked all around. I thought to myself, 'Who on earth are they? What do they want?' I had never seen them before. Soon Martin came on the scene and a great conversation seemed to take place. I became uneasy, so like any other woman I went out to investigate.

I was introduced to both men, who were very well dressed,

with suit, shirt and tie. One was called Mr Alan Davidson from Portadown, and the other man was the late Mr George Marshall from Lurgan.

These two men were on a mission and wanted to achieve what God had directed them to do, which was to bring the glorious message of the gospel to the people living in Ashfield and the surrounding areas.

What a challenge for anyone, but what a tremendous responsibility! Both these men were saved by God's grace some years previously and were in happy fellowship in assemblies of God's people.

We read in 2nd Timothy 4:2 of the faithfulness in preaching the word of God - "Preach the word; be instant in season, out of season; reprove, rebuke, exhort with all longsuffering and doctrine." When I realised what their exercise and intentions were, to erect a portable hall in our yard and invite friends, family and neighbours to hear the message of the gospel, I was extremely pleased and I was ready to assist them whenever needed. Martin and I prayed earnestly that God's hand would be seen in the salvation of souls at this time.

The time came when the erection of the hall took place. Our girls were so excited they actually went out to watch how a few men could complete such an incredible building in such a short space of time and even tried to give a helping hand. My youngest daughter, Martine, was also present but didn't really understand the determination of willpower of these men and what their intentions were, but was happy just to sit on the bottom step of the ladder and watch.

Many invitations and gospel tracts were distributed from door to door, inviting people to attend. Transport was available if needed. The gospel meetings commenced and many in the district attended quite often. This was very encouraging to both Martin and me, and the two preachers. These two men really did get help each night to sow the good seed of the

Wooden hut in our yard for the gospel to be preached

gospel, how a sinner could come in burdened down with a load of sins and could leave with the burden gone. What better news could fall on anyone's ears? The Scriptures very clearly outline the fact that we are not saved as the result of our own works, righteous acts or efforts. In fact, according to God's word, our own efforts or merits have nothing at all to do with our salvation. God does not take any of them into account.

I love to hear that beautiful hymn sung:

> 'Twas Jesus, my Saviour, who died on the tree,
> To open a fountain for sinners like me;
> His blood is that fountain which pardon bestows,
> And cleanses the foulest wherever it flows.
>
> Come, sinners, to Jesus! no longer delay!
> A full free salvation He offers today,
> Arouse your dark spirits, awake from your dream,
> And Christ will support you in coming to Him.

65

For the conquering Saviour shall break every chain,
And give us the victory again and again.

Henry Q Wilson

It had now come to the last night of the preaching of the gospel in the wooden hall in our yard and I felt very sad as I had high hopes of seeing more blessing in salvation. God was good in saving a soul a young lad of around ten years of age. Soon the hall was dismantled and removed, and this left an empty feeling. It affected me to think of the gospel having been brought to our very door. Satan, the devil, was very active in removing the good seed of the gospel for he knows that time is short. "The coming of the Lord draweth nigh." We read in Luke 21 of signs of coming events. Revelation 22:20 says, "Surely I come quickly," – there will be no time then to prepare - opportunity gone, not ready.

A few years later we had the great privilege of offering our yard to two local brethren to erect another wooden hall to preach the same gospel. These meetings were also well attended and God's hand was seen in blessing in salvation. Those who professed faith in Christ at that time are today strong witnesses of the reality of God's 'so great salvation'.

We read God's words in John 10:28 - "My sheep hear my voice, and I know them, and they follow me: And I give unto them eternal life; and they shall never perish, neither shall any man pluck them out of my hand." What a security for the believer!

Chapter 5

My Mother's Death

My mother was getting frail and I could see her becoming physically weaker. She was now unable to do things for herself. It terrified me to see my mother deteriorating so rapidly. In the year of 1989, due to her ill health, she had to be admitted to Banbridge Hospital for nursing care. There she received all the help she needed in the closing days and hours of her life. I visited my mother quite often and I was with her in her last moments. As she lay there in the bed, in all her weakness, I could see by her lips that she was trying to say something. I put my ear down to her mouth and in a distant whisper I heard words that she had sang many, many times. Here are the words:

> We're travelling home to Heaven above,
> Will you go? Will you go?
> To sing the Saviour's dying love,
> Will you go? Will you go?
> Millions have reached that blissful shore,
> Their trials and their labours o'er,
> And yet there's room for millions more,
> Will you go? Will you go?
>
> The way to Heaven is straight and plain:
> Will you go? Will you go?
> Repent, believe, be born again.
> Will you go? Will you go?
> The Saviour cries aloud to thee,
> Take up thy cross and follow Me,

And thou shalt My salvation see.
Will you go? Will you go?

O could I hear some sinner say -
I will go! I will go!
From Christ I can no longer stay!
I will go! I will go!
My old companions, fare ye well,
I will not go with you to Hell:
I mean with Jesus Christ to dwell,
I will go! I will go!

Richard Jukes (1804–67)

It was on the 18th February 1990 that my dear mother, named Eva May, passed away into the presence of her Lord and Saviour. My mother's remains were brought to our home for burial. This was an extremely sad time for us all. However, I was very thankful that I was able to set a letter on the hall table which was handwritten by my late mother, relating her personal testimony. Everyone who called in our home was able to read it for themselves.

Here is part of her testimony in her own words.
It was while attending special gospel meetings in Shanaghan Gospel Hall in the year of 1934 I got saved. These meetings were conducted by the late Mr Samuel S M Curran and Mr William Bunting – both evangelists. 1 Peter 2:24 was the verse used by God in my salvation. It says, "Who his own self bare our sins in his own body on the tree, that we, being dead to sins, should live unto righteousness, by whose stripes ye are healed." I accepted Christ as my own and personal Saviour.

The funeral service was conducted by two well-known evangelists, Mr Bobby Eadie and the late Mr Jim Hutchinson, and shared with the Rev. D Priestly, Free Presbyterian Church, Banbridge. I requested the hymn 'We're travelling home to

Heaven above', which was so dear to my late mother, to be sung just before her remains were taken from our home for burial.

When one loses a mother they lose a very special person in their lives. She is the one that keeps all the family together. A mother is always the centre of the home.

Silver Wedding Anniversary

Three weeks after my mother's funeral it was our silver wedding anniversary, which was on the 10th March 1990. My four daughters, family and friends worked hard to make our special event a success. We had a meal in the White Gables Hotel in Hillsborough. I had been married for twenty-five years to a man who was my soulmate, my best ever friend, my loving, caring husband, Martin. However, there was a deep sadness because there were those who were missing: my mother, father and Martin's father. It was a lovely evening and many photographs were taken. One that still hangs on the wall in our living room is of my two brothers, William and John, my two sisters, Mary and Jean, and me. Little did I know that this photograph would be the last one taken of the five of us together.

Just eleven days later, on the 21st March 1990, I received a phone call from my sister-in-law, Margaret, to inform me that my dear brother, William, had taken a severe heart attack and died suddenly. I was overcome by this news and I found it very hard to accept that, once again, another member of our family, only fifty-two years of age, had been taken from us in a moment of time. A wife left without a husband and two girls left without a father.

My brother's death left a great impression on my life. Martin found it hard to accept this sudden news. He had lost a brother-in-law, one that worked so hard with him in the building trade.

Changes took place in our home. Martin left the building trade and, through time, built up his own business in farming. He always had a great interest in cattle, sheep and sows with little piglets, from when he was a schoolboy. He had been often found around the farms of his neighbours, helping out with their everyday duties. Martin also liked to visit the cattle markets in Dromore, Markethill, Rathfriland, Banbridge and Dungannon.

I can remember Martin buying his first cattle lorry. I thought it looked like such a huge vehicle. Driving a cattle lorry was not always sunshine, but he always put a great effort into all that he was doing, especially when working with the public. He was meeting new faces each day around the cattle markets. He spent many late nights delivering animals to the farmers, but I greatly admired him for putting the Lord's work as his first priority. He attended the Tuesday night weekly prayer meeting and the Thursday night weekly Bible reading, a meeting for the study of the Scriptures. Sometime later Martin built a cattle shed in our yard to store cows ready for calving. When Martin was away driving his lorry I was left in charge, so when a cow was giving birth I had to deliver. However, I soon got used to it. Martin and I worked as a team and if we needed assistance, help was near at hand. We were blessed with good neighbours who were only a phone call away.

Martine began to get stronger and even with her disabilities she started to walk. Nothing pleased her as much as when I would set her up into the cab of the lorry beside her daddy to go to deliver cattle, sheep or lambs to their destinations. Martine was an outside girl.

Pamela's Nursing Career

When my eldest daughter, Pamela, became the age to take up employment, she decided she would like to enter the nursing profession. This meant she had to leave us to take up residence at the Musgrave Park Hospital, Belfast, but she would come home on her off duty days. Martin and I were delighted to see her and we spent much of our time chatting about things in general. We soon got used to her absence around the house.

One weekend when she came home from her duties she informed her father and I that she now had a boyfriend. His name was Maurice Russell, who also was a farmer, and he came from as far away as Killinchy, Comber. Were we to watch this space? Time would tell.

Holiday in Menorca

It was now summer 1991. Time was passing quickly and Pamela and Maurice had started to make plans for their forthcoming wedding, which was to be in May 1992.

With Pamela being away from home, Martin and I thought it would be nice, if at all possible, to take her and our youngest daughter, Martine, on a holiday in the sun. We talked it over with the family. At this time Sharon was now working with John Graham's Contractors, Dromore, and Amanda was working in Cottage Catering, also in Dromore.

Pamela informed us that she had been given one week annual leave in mid-August. I was excited at the idea. This would likely be our last holiday together before the wedding. The question asked was, "Where will we go?" So off we went to the travel agents in Banbridge, and after pondering over many brochures we decided to spend one week in a hotel apartment in a resort called Cala'n Forcat, Menorca.

Cala'n Forcat, Menorca was renowned for its unspoilt countryside and the lovely shore where you could swim from one beautiful beach to the next. This was just Pamela's scene as she loved to swim and soak up the sun.

Our hotel apartment was amazing. Beside our apartment a barbecue was held each night by the pool. We had the pleasure of going to a festival in Mahon, the capital of Menorca. There I had the joy of seeing many palm trees lining the promenade and lots of floats and flowers. The night before we were due to leave for home, we were sitting having a chat beside the pool and we met a young married couple from Dromore. As we got into conversation, I soon learned that the young lady, Pamela and I had something in common - we are all nurses. We really did enjoy the banter. Unknown to me, this same nurse was to attend to my needs after my surgery in 1995. She is now the district nursing sister in our area. Truly I can say, "As for God, His way is perfect".

Pamela's Wedding

On 30th May 1992, we had our first wedding. I well remember that morning. I thought everything was going according to plan. The three bridesmaids and the little flowergirl were all dressed and ready to go. I was dressed, but feeling quite nervous, as I watched for the taxi to arrive to take us to Mullafernaghan Gospel Hall, Banbridge, for the wedding, which was due to take place at 12 noon.

Our daughter Pamela's wedding

Guests at Pamela's wedding:
Front L to R: Florence Bradford, Stephanie Bradford
Mrs Mary Megaw, Bride's Mum, Mrs Jean Harbinson
Back: John Bradford, Sydney Megaw, Bride's Dad,
William Harbinson (all related)

With the time approaching, I could see Martin becoming anxious. Soon the taxis arrived. Was everything in order as planned? We all thought so. As I gazed at Pamela, the bride, I thought she looked beautiful, but one thing she had forgotten about was her veil. Where was her veil? There was a great commotion in the Beggs' home that morning! We searched everywhere for it, or as I would say, the house was ransacked trying to find her veil. I was panic-stricken as the search continued. Someone came up with the idea of phoning the bridal shop in Newtownards, and tell them what had happened. Time was running out. Pamela was very upset, but she knew this was her last chance to find out about her missing veil.

She went to the phone and with an anxious voice spoke to the lady from whom she had bought the dress. By this time it was midday. I could hear her say to Pamela to calm down and search inside the covering which had been over her wedding dress. Sure enough, there it was, all bundled up in a ball, stuck in the corner. Phew, what a relief! The iron was brought out and the veil made ready for Pamela to wear. The panic was over.

By the time we got to the Gospel Hall all my anxiety soon disappeared. The hall was filled to capacity and the crowd of onlookers was unbelievable. Mr Albert Aiken (evangelist) officiated. Albert made one statement which has never left me. Here are the words: "Those who pray together, stay together." I thought to myself that it was good advice to a young Christian couple starting out together into a world full of corruption and wickedness. They both settled into their new home in Killinchy, Comber.

My Final Holiday in London

It was my 50th birthday on 2nd December 1994. This was a big milestone for me and I didn't want any fuss, but my two daughters, Sharon and Amanda, were having none of this. So to my delight and much excitement they clubbed together and bought me a ticket for a trip to London for a long weekend.

We got up on Thursday morning, packed our bags and off we went to Belfast International Airport at Aldergrove, leaving Martin and Martine at home. We boarded the plane laughing and joking, keeping the stewards going. It was so much fun.

We arrived at Heathrow and the place was buzzing because it was near Christmas. It was full of Christmas trees and Christmas carols were playing. It just looked amazing. We headed for the tube station and there we were, jumping from one train to another!

Finally, we arrived at the Royal Court Hotel, right in the middle of London where all the shops, cafes, restaurants etc.

are. We checked in and got the key to our room. Oh, the excitement! We just couldn't wait to get to the shops.

Two days were spent laughing, shopping, eating, losing one another in the shops, spending money, meeting the famous Bruce Forsythe in Harrods and getting told off for taking pictures. Oh my, the fun that we had! Our joy soon turned to fear and tears when we were told before we boarded the plane to Belfast International Airport that the weather was not good and we were going to hit some air pockets.

About twenty minutes into our return journey the plane started to sway from side to side. We had flown into a really bad thunderstorm with forked lightning and really heavy rain. Our journey that night took a little bit longer and we had to circle around in the sky for what seemed like hours because it was too dangerous for us land. Thankfully, after some prayer, we were given the go-ahead to land. My two daughters and I were never as glad to see the ground in all our lives. God was good and saw us safely back home that night to be with Martin and Martine. This was a very happy, energetic and excitement-filled holiday for me, but little did I know it was to be my last ever holiday involving a plane trip.

The Accident

Martin was still using his lorry each day, delivering cattle to the different markets. The year was 1995 and things were about to change for our family. I can recall one Friday morning that Martin was booked by one of our neighbours to take his cattle to the Rathfriland Co-op to sell. On his arrival at the farm to load the cattle, tragedy struck and the dear farmer lost his life in a freak accident.

When I visited the scene I did all that was possible to give first aid to the wounded man, but it was all over in the matter of minutes. My heart sank in despair. It was unbelievable that this could happen to a highly respected farmer with our cattle lorry, driven by my husband, Martin.

Martin and I, and indeed all my family, friends and neighbours from the farming community, were devastated to lose such an extremely good friend and a great neighbour. We did ask, "Why?" God allowed it to happen, which is beyond our control. It is God that holds our very breath in his hands. He knows every heartbeat, pulse rate, thoughts and all our deep trials. This is why it is most important to be saved at an early age for 'tomorrow is eternity, just hidden from our view.' After a few weeks passed I became very depressed because I was getting flashbacks of what had taken place.

Chapter 6

Unexpected News

As the new year of 1995 commenced many people were complaining of having colds and flu-like symptoms. I took a sore throat and became unwell. Being a nurse, I tried all the well-known home cure remedies but to no avail. I then decided to visit my local G.P. Soon an appointment was made and I was on my way to the surgery. After taking two courses of antibiotics my condition was no better, but rather got worse. My weight appeared to be gradually dropping and my appetite was now becoming poor. It had got to the stage that I found it difficult to swallow food as my throat seemed to be closing in.

After four months of agonising pain and discomfort my frustration was unbelievable. At this point my emotional response was, "Does anyone really understand how I feel?" I knew within myself that something was drastically wrong. What was I to do? By this time I had lost two stone in weight and my family was desperate. My last hope was to be referred to an ENT (ear, nose and throat) specialist at the Royal Victoria Hospital, Belfast.

My consultant, Mr Primrose, held a clinic one day a week in the Lagan Valley Hospital, Lisburn, and it was here that I had my first consultation with him. I found him to be a very sympathetic and caring doctor. A few tests and x-rays were done and in a very short space of time I was called for my results. I had throat cancer.

Many Christians visited me in my own home and sought to

comfort me by reading from the Scriptures and bringing my every need to God in prayer, that whatever God had laid out for me I would receive the strength and courage to accept. Now my faith in God, in whom I had put my trust many years previously, was to be tested and tried.

It had come to the stage that I had to face up to the reality of the unpleasant fact. A word no one wants to hear is cancer. I had cancer of the throat. What a terrible shock to the system! I had nursed many patients with cancer, but when I was actually given the diagnosis from my consultant, my first reaction straight away was, 'I'm going to die.' I did ask the question, "Why me, Lord?" I wasn't a smoker or a drinker of alcohol, yet this word, cancer, was never to leave me.

A further appointment was made for me to attend the outpatients' clinic at the ENT department at the Royal Victoria Hospital, Belfast. My family accompanied me for support. As I sat in the chair, waiting for my name to be called for a consultation with my consultant, a cancer doctor and a nurse specialist, many things entered my head. I went into a state of despair; my heart became heavy as I now had to face up to reality. What were they going to say?

As we entered the little room my family and I were very anxious, but I knew they would be with me, no matter the outcome. This growth in my throat had to be removed. At this stage my throat was becoming worse. I now had difficulties swallowing food.

My Decision

At this stage in my life I felt the presence of the Lord with me. A few Scripture verses were impressed on my mind. They are found in the book of Proverbs 3:5,6 - "Trust in the Lord with all thine heart; and lean not unto thine own understanding. In all thy ways acknowledge him, and he shall direct thy paths."

I was given two options. The first option was treatment, but with no guarantee of any shrinkage of the growth in my throat. The second option was to have surgery to have it removed, but because of where it was situated my voice box would also have to be removed, leaving me with total loss of speech. This news that was given to me was unbelievable. My mind stopped thinking. Was this all a very bad dream? No, it was real. The team of experts left the room, leaving me and my family to talk and try to come to a decision. We were all scared. Each one gave me their points of view, but I could not make any headway myself.

Just then, Pamela said, "Mummy, you are the only one who can make the decision, and no matter what, we, as a family, are all behind you." We sat there waiting. As the door opened and in came Mr Primrose, my consultant, and the other cancer specialist doctor, I started to tremble and my eyes filled with tears. I cried within myself, "Lord, what will You have me to do?" At this point I felt a measure of confidence and knew that whatever the Lord had in store for me, it would be in the mind and will of God.

The big question came to me from my consultant, Mr Primrose. "Myrtle, it is now up to you to give us your final decision." I hesitated for a while, looking at Mr Primrose with tear-filled eyes. My response was, as the Lord had led me to say, "I'll go with the surgery." Mr Primrose looked at me with tears in his own eyes and said, "I think you have made the right choice." All I wanted at this stage was to be free from this growth in my throat. I cannot remember much more that was said, as my mind became overwrought. I now had to wait for a date, a time, and a bed so that I could be admitted to Ward 29 ENT at the Royal Victoria Hospital.

On my return home, news soon spread about the serious and pending operation. The visits and prayers of the Lord's dear people again gave me great help and comfort. The Scriptures were opened and read in my presence again, lifting my name up to the only comforter, my Lord and Saviour, Christ Jesus.

We read in the Scriptures in James 5:15,16 that "the prayer of faith shall save the sick, and the Lord shall raise him up...The effectual fervent prayer of a righteous man availeth much." I had been given many Scriptures to read myself. One that stayed with me was Psalm 118:5-9.

The time came when I received a phone call to confirm the date and time when I was to be admitted to Ward 29 ENT at the Royal Victoria Hospital. The morning came for me to say farewell to friends and neighbours. Off I went in the car, with Martin and my daughters, to face an unknown future, but a future which was known by God. The date was 25th June 1995. Many things filled my mind as I left my beautiful home at Ashfield. I took great pride and delight in our garden with all the lovely flowers and shrubs. Most were starting to develop with buds and some were out in full bloom. I loved gardening and on a warm, sunny day when little or no rain had fallen, it was always my delight to attend to all the shrubs, keeping them well watered and fed, otherwise they would wither and eventually die. This reminded me of myself. Here I was, once a cheerful, shining individual and a helper, friend and listening ear for those who were in deep trials and facing problems. I was only a telephone call away and help was given.

As darkness started to overshadow my mind, what was I to do? No-one could help me at this point in my life. I realised now that I needed spiritual help and nourishment for my own soul, otherwise how was I going to survive? My mind was directed to the book of Psalms and there in Psalm 33:18,19 these words were impressed on my mind - "Behold, the eye of the Lord is upon them that fear him, upon them that hope in his mercy; to deliver their soul from death, and to keep them alive in famine." God also sees those who trust in Him for salvation and who depend on His mercy for provision. These are the ones who please Him. He looks down on them with keenest favour. "I will lift up mine eyes unto the hills, from whence cometh my help. My help cometh from the Lord, which made Heaven and earth" (Psalm 121:1,2). Even with all these Scriptures in my mind I still remained in a trance-like state. I cannot recall my journey to hospital that day.

Admitted to Ward 29 ENT

I was admitted to Ward 29 ENT. Martin and my daughters left me in the care of Mr Primrose and all his caring and sympathetic nursing staff. Tears flowed freely from my eyes as we said our goodbyes. Many thoughts filled my mind. Would ever I survive to be allowed home to be with my family and friends again?

The morning came for me to have my operation. I can remember going to the telephone to speak to Martin, and with a very hoarse throat I told him, "I love you." This was to be the last time he would hear me speak with my voice. If I did not survive, I would meet him in Heaven. Martin tried to comfort me, saying, "God is in control. Just leave all in His hands." Again tears streamed down my cheeks as I could detect from Martin's voice that he was heartbroken. We then had to say our goodbyes. It was very, very hard and distressing. Here I was, again feeling a great sense of loneliness and abandonment.

I soon returned to my ward to await my time to go to theatre for my surgery. My mind was drawn to those words written in Scripture. I lifted my Bible, or as I would call it, 'my sword', opened it at Psalm 118:6-8 and started to read. "The Lord is on my side; I will not fear: what can man do unto me? The Lord taketh my part with them that help me...It is better to trust in the Lord than to put confidence in man." From that moment onward I got great comfort to know that God was now in full control. I knew that many Christians, both from here in Northern Ireland and in many countries around the world, were praying for me, lifting up their voices to the God of Heaven that my operation would be a success and that I would be raised up to a measure of health and strength and be able to come to terms with change.

My operation required three teams of doctors - my ENT consultant, Mr Bill Primrose, an oncologist, Doctor Russell Houston, and a thoracic surgeon, Mr Ashor Tewary - to work together to perform my operation. This was major surgery, as I had to have my pharynx, larynx, oesophagus and one thyroid gland, plus two parathyroid glands removed. My stomach had to be relocated higher up within my chest area. This was to leave me with a permanent laryngectomy and total loss of speech. I spent a period of time in the Intensive Care Unit at the Royal Victoria Hospital before I was transferred to Ward 29 again.

When I began to come round after the general anaesthetic, I can clearly remember opening my eyes and seeing only the four walls in my own single ward. A nurse was sitting by my bedside. I tried to speak but there was no sound. I would never be able to speak with my own voice ever again on this side of eternity. As time passed, soon both my lungs collapsed and my survival rate was critical. By this stage my husband and family were told that I had stage two squamous cell carcinoma of the pharynx, larynx and oesophagus. This left a dark shadow over them regarding my recovery.

As my future was in the balance I made contact with an evangelist, a preacher of the gospel, one whom I had known for years, regarding my funeral arrangements. However, with all the professional care I received from my consultant, doctors and all the nursing staff and the treatments I was given, my condition improved slightly after a few days.

As drains and drips were slowly removed over a period of time, the realisation started to dawn upon my mind. Some of my family were now allowed to visit me. This was a very emotional time for us all. They would read the Scriptures to me, but had to be alert and careful not to ask me any questions. My daughter brought me a notepad and pen, which was my only means of communication. Indeed, it was as if I had gone back to my childhood days – I was back to reading and writing.

My family and I went into a state of shock and a period of grieving. I had lost my voice, something we all take for granted, to talk with and sing with. No one knew how frustrating and depressing this situation was for me. As a result of my operation I was left with no smell and my only means of breathing was through a hole in my lower throat. I was being fed through tubes which were attached to my abdomen. This continued for some weeks.

As I started to make slow progress, some of the clips were removed from my neck wound. It was now time for me to receive a visit from the speech therapist. I found her to be a caring, friendly and supportive lady who sought to teach me how to use an artificial servox, which is an electronic speech device with intone. It was easy to handle and easy to charge the batteries in a charging unit.

I got a little stronger and soon I was free from drips and tubes. However, unfortunately, due to an outbreak of an infectious disease in the ward known as MRSA, one of the wounds in my abdomen became infected, leaving me with no other option but to be nursed in an isolation ward. At this time my family were very concerned about my condition. Here I was - I had been making good progress and now this terrible setback. These words came to my mind and I knew they were from the Lord:

When the storms of life are raging,
Tempests wild on sea and land,
I will seek a place of refuge
In the shadow of God's hand.

He will hide me! He will hide me!
Where no harm...can e'er betide me;
He will hide me! safely hide me
In the shadow of His hand.

Though He may send some afflictions,
'Twill but make me long for home;
For in love and not in anger,
All His chastenings will come.

Enemies may strive to injure,
Satan all his arts employ;
God will turn what seems to harm me
Into everlasting joy.

So, while here the cross I'm bearing,
Meeting storms and billows wild,
Jesus for my soul is caring,
Naught can harm His Father's child.

M E Servoss

My First Letter

It was a hot Monday morning and I felt warm and clammy.
The electric fans were going and the windows were opened
slightly. After having my dressings changed, the nurses set
me out in the chair for a short period of time. I was very
weak and as I sat there my eyes started to wander about the
room. The get well cards, that my family had put up on the
wall with blue-tac, caught my eye. That morning I counted
a total of seventy-four 'get well' cards and there were many
more to follow.

The nurses were great, and as time passed I got to know
some of them individually. They were always there for me,
no matter what I wanted. As I sat in the chair that morning

my mind eventually went to my family at home in Ashfield. All of them had been a great help to me along my difficult journey. Martin visited me daily, sometimes twice daily, and did his work in between. How was I going to let them know my feelings about them? My notebook and pen were sitting on my bedside locker and when I got settled I made my thoughts known to Barbara, who was a Christian nurse. Her words to me were, "Myrtle, in your own time, when your concentration and your mind become clearer, take your notebook and pen and write to Martin and the girls to let them know how much you have appreciated all that they have done for you. When you have finished, just give it to me and I will see that your family receive it. Just you do the writing and I will do the delivery. Myrtle, just trust me."

Those words spoken to me by Barbara, "Just trust me," brought my memory back to that moment, now some forty-nine years ago, when those words became a great blessing to me as I put my trust in Christ who delivered me out of darkness into light. We read in 1 John 2:8, "I write unto you, which thing is true in him and in you: because the darkness is past, and the true light now shineth." Christ is the true light, always shining, and whenever sinners turn to Him, they shall be saved and henceforth love their fellow believers. The hymn writer penned it well.

> Trust and obey;
> For there's no other way
> To be happy in Jesus,
> But to trust and obey.

It took me quite a while to get a few lines put together. However, I got it finished and Barbara was true to her word and got it delivered to my family.

I now had to wait to hear if I required any further treatment, such as chemotherapy or radiotherapy. I learned later that the margins were clear, but they could not guarantee that the cancer cells hadn't spread. At this point in time I would not have been fit for treatment due to weakness and my physical state. I had already spent thirteen and a half weeks in Ward 29 at the Royal Victoria Hospital.

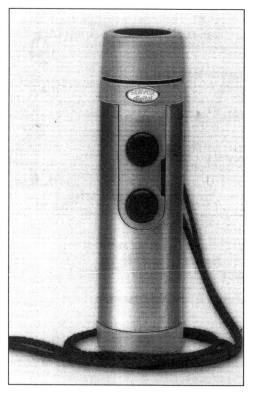

My Servox. My only means of speech at the press of a button from June 1995 until today 2015

Chapter 7

Leaving Hospital

It was now time for me to leave hospital. I was to leave all the caring staff who were so faithful to me and my family by helping and giving me good advice. How was I to manage or cope with difficulties? I must confess that I had mixed feelings about leaving. I was now being exposed to the outside world. Just before I left Ward 29, I had the great privilege to go around many of the patients, telling them, by using my wee machine (servox), what the Lord had done for me, as a Christian saved by the grace of God many years previously. It was my faith in God that brought me through some of the darkest days in my life. The hymn says:

> I have nothing to do with tomorrow,
> My Saviour will make that His care,
> It may be filled with teardrops and heartache
> He will help us to suffer and bear.

Going Home – Fear and Dread

This was a new way of living for me, my family and friends. Life seemed so uncertain. I felt afraid. How was I going to cope with change in the outside world? Was I going to be a burden to my family? Unknown to me, my family were told I might only survive a year.

I was still an ill woman requiring daily dressings to my wounds. These had to be done by a team of district nurses. I had also the Macmillan nurses, my own GP and carers who helped me and encouraged me on a daily basis, as well as all my family. By this time my weight had dropped below seven stone. I had many problems which arose from having had a laryngectomy, including being very prone to chest infections.

With the very warm summer, my family thought it would be nice to take me up to Portstewart for a few days, thinking perhaps the sea air would be of some benefit to me. I was only home from hospital a fortnight when all the arrangements were made. I had mixed feelings about all of this because my wounds required daily dressings.

My daughter, Pamela, a qualified nurse, was well aware of my condition. Martin had rented a lovely house in Portstewart near the sea front. Everything looked beautiful, the sea was calm and the beach was crowded. What a scene! I thought this was very different from what I had been used to over the last few months in Ward 29 ENT in the Royal Victoria Hospital.

After our first night there, I became quite sick and the family had to send for the doctor on call. When the doctor arrived I was so sick that I had to be transferred by ambulance back to Ward 29. I was to spend the next two weeks there to recuperate. This was to be an ongoing thing for me over the next year or so as I was very prone to infections, including chest infections.

I spent some time at Craigavon Area Hospital to recover. I was still attending the ENT outpatients department at the Royal Victoria Hospital to see Mr Primrose. This took place every two months until I finally reached the one year mark.

One thing which disturbed me and really tried my patience was when the telephone rang. Through time, my family and the Macmillan nurses helped me to pluck up the courage to answer it when it rang. So I decided to have a go. When I did, I felt great and I got over my first hurdle. It was an advantage for me to communicate with the outside world. As the weeks passed, I regained confidence in myself.

One morning on answering the telephone I said, "Hello," and to my shock I heard a female voice trying to imitate me and mock me. She laughed and made funny remarks on the telephone. I tried to explain as best I could that this was the only method by which I could speak. However, she did not want to know. Still she continued on, thinking this was all a funny joke. I put the telephone down and I was left frustrated, disappointed, discouraged and disgusted. This was a very big setback for both me and my family and put me into a bout of depression.

As I went to bed that night I was very disheartened. I can well remember awakening up from sleep in the middle of the night and beginning to have suicidal thoughts. I switched on the light and lifted my Bible, and to my amazement it opened in my favourite book of the Bible – the Psalms. Psalm 46:10 was revealed to me - "Be still, and know that I am God." I found at this time that God's word was my only consolation and an encouragement to my soul.

Our New Millennium Shop

In the year 1999, Martin carefully considered his future in farming, with much prayer and exercise before the Lord. His desire was to spend as much time with me as possible. Historically, there had been a shop at Ashfield which included a local Post Office but unfortunately these had had to close as the owners retired from the business. 'Ashfield Stores', as it was then known, opened in the year 1920 by the late Mr Adam Poots. It was then run by his daughters, Evelyn, Paxie and Rachel, known as Ray. I got to know these three ladies and spent much time in their company. This store sold a wide range of items such as drapery, hardware, boots and shoes. They also had a good coal and meal trade.

Our Millennium Shop
L to R: owner - Martin, daughters (Amanda, Sharon, Martine)
and Myrtle

Back in those days, the local store was also the meeting place for farmers and locals to have a chat, while their groceries were made up to be delivered in their famous blue van. Most of the customers back then had what was called a 'grocery book'. This book was a small, hard backed book which was used to list their groceries. In those days many had to walk to their nearest stores to order their groceries.

In the year of 1989, Ray, being the only surviving member, shut up shop. Beside the shop was the Post Office, owned and run by the McCrum family. It too was to close its doors due to the owners' retirement in 1989. Martin and I often talked about the shops at the corner. We missed them both. Martin came up with the idea of building a shop in our yard, provided he could get planning permission.

The Lord opened up the way and we got our planning permission through to build a shop. Martin opted out of farming to start a new venture. The shop was built and it was opened by the late Mr David McCrum. As the ribbon was cut, David said that his desire was that Martin's new millennium shop, known now as Ashwood Country Shop, would be a very successful business in the days and years that lay ahead, DV. I was presented by one of our neighbours with two blue plant pots, each of which had a lovely plant. I thought they were both beautiful and I set them in front of the shop for everyone to see.

Our business started to develop and grow. Martin's mother, Elizabeth, took a great interest in the shop and her desire was that her eldest son would be successful in his new business. She was delighted and proud to be at the official opening. Unfortunately, the shop was only opened a few weeks when news came to us that Elizabeth had died in the quietness of the night. This was on the 9th May 2000. Martin and I were in total shock. Soon the shutters of the shop were pulled down and a notice put on the door – 'Closed due to a Family Bereavement.' People were seen coming to the shop to get their groceries, but found the door was shut.

When I thought of such an incident, my mind suddenly went to a verse in the Scriptures which speaks of another door. This door is still open, but it could close at any moment - it is the door to Heaven. John 10:9 is one of those delightful verses which is simple enough for the Sunday school pupil to understand and yet can never be exhausted by the most learned scholars. The Lord Jesus Christ is speaking. "I am the door: by me if any man enter in, he shall be saved, and shall go in and out, and find pasture." We must enter in by Christ and live by the power which He gives.

The day of the funeral was from Elizabeth's late home in Wallace Park, Dromore, to the new cemetery in Banbridge. Mr Jack Lennox from Magherafelt was responsible to speak at the service.

<u>Fishing</u>

I spent many days in bed due to my illness. One day I would feel quite good, the next day saw me depressed due to my low immune system. I was weak and very vulnerable and exposed to attacks on my mind, especially from Satan, the devil. As I lay there in my sick bed thoughts would penetrate my mind. However, I often thought of how the Lord had preserved me over so many years. He has sustained, supported and provided for me each time I was in distress. I was always mindful to take heed and follow God's word. What had the Lord in store for me? In Mark 1:16-18 we are given Mark's account of what took place by the Sea of Galilee. Jesus saw Simon and Andrew fishing. He had met them before. In fact, they had become His disciples at the outset of His ministry (John 1:40,41). Now He called them to be with Him, promising to make them 'fishers of men'. It says that they immediately gave up their lucrative fishing business to follow Him. Their obedience was prompt, sacrificial and complete. This tells me:

- Fishing is an art, and so is soul winning.
- It requires patience.
- Often there are lonely hours of waiting.
- It requires skill in the use of bait, lines or nets.
- It requires discernment and common sense in going where the fish are running.
- It requires persistence; a good fisherman is not easy discouraged.
- It requires quietness. The best policy is to avoid disturbance and to keep self in the background.
- When a person accepts Christ as their Saviour, each one becomes fishers of men by following Christ.

The more like Him we are, the more successful we will be in winning others to Him. One does not have to be a great preacher, or an articulate speaker. The following words then came to my mind - "Is there anything I can do to reach out to those who have no time to think of eternal matters?"

Throughout my life I always had a great desire to help others, especially those passing through trials due to the loss of a loved one or sickness. With me having total loss of speech I prayed to God that I would be led by the Spirit of God and would be obedient to His will.

Car Stolen

In the year of 2001 many cars were reported to be stolen in and around our area. Unfortunately, we also became victims. Our Mercedes car that was parked at the side of the shop was taken by thieves. This was a great setback for me and my family. I had some personal documents in the car, including my blue disabled badge, my exemption card from wearing a seatbelt, a new coat and Martin's most treasured Bible. We never got our car back. However, Martin's Bible was found lying in the ditch some distance up the road.

It was now time for me to attend the Outpatients ENT at the Royal Victoria Hospital to see Mr Primrose. On our way home, Martin was driving the newly acquired car on the dual carriageway. When we came to the turnoff for Dromore, a police car passed us with the flashers and siren going. This really frightened me. It pulled in front of us and the policeman waved us down. My first thoughts were, "What on earth have we done?" We pulled in to the side of the road. A policeman got out, put on his hat and brought out his notebook and pen, ready for action. His manner of speech was unpleasant to the both of us. He asked Martin why he was not wearing his seatbelt. He did admit that he had overlooked it and knew that he had broken the law. The police officer went over some ritual saying before he handed Martin a penalty fine. Then it was my turn.

He came round to my door and said, "Madam, why are you not wearing your seatbelt?" I could not speak. However, I struggled to look for my servox. Martin saw the state of my frustration so he tried to explain to him that I had been exempt from wearing a seatbelt for over six years. We both knew straightaway by his attitude towards us that he did not believe us. Martin informed the officer that his previous car had been stolen and all my documents were in it, including my exemption card. I started to cry. The situation that I was in became unbearable. I remembered that I had, in my handbag, a letter from my own doctor stating that I was exempt from wearing a seatbelt dated back to when I had my operation some years previously. To my surprise, after he read it he handed it back to me. It did not seem to matter. I had no other option but to accept a penalty fine.

After we returned home we started to discuss all that had taken place. Many thoughts filled my mind. The events of the day were going through my mind and I couldn't think properly. Satan was trying to fill my mind so that I did not have the same appetite for God's word. However, God overruled in my confused circumstances. The words of the hymn, written by Edward Wakefield, which I had often heard sung, became sweet to me:

> Press forward and fear not, the billows may roll.
> But the power of Jesus their rage can control;
> Though waves rise in anger, their tumult shall cease;
> One word of His bidding shall hush them to peace.
>
> Press forward and fear not; though trial be near;
> The Lord is our refuge - whom then, shall we fear?
> His staff is our comfort, our safeguard His rod!
> Then let us be steadfast and trust in our God.
>
> Press forward and fear not; be strong in the Lord,
> In the power of His promise, the truth of His word;
> Through the sea and the desert our pathway may tend,
> But He who hath saved us will save to the end.
>
> Press forward and fear not; we'll speed on our way;
> Why should we e'er shrink from our path in dismay?
> We tread but the road which our leader has trod;
> Then let us press forward, and trust in our God.

Changes Again in Our Family

Shortly after this, our third daughter Amanda, who had been engaged to a young man called Wayne Copeland, from Donaghcloney, informed us that they had decided to get married in six weeks' time. Amanda always said that if ever she was to get married she would go quietly with no fuss. This was in the beginning of July 2001 and the date of the wedding was to be the 25th August 2001.

Amanda's wedding L to R: Gareth (Bestman), Wayne (Groom), Amanda (Bride), Martine (Bridesmaid)

Amanda was working in our shop and took it all in her stride. She had all the arrangements made on time. The day came and the weather was dry. Martin had an old vintage car ordered to take both him and Amanda to the registry office in Banbridge. It was a brilliant day and I really enjoyed the venue. Amanda was now married and had set up home with her husband, Wayne, in the village of Donaghcloney.

A few months passed and we were now into a new year. It was 12th January 2002. Martin was standing in the shop, just before 9:00am on a Saturday morning, when our daughter, Sharon, rang to tell him that his first grandchild was born. He was so delighted to hear that he had a little granddaughter to add to the family, and everybody who came through the door that day was told about his little granddaughter, Chloe Elizabeth, who was named after his mother.

Six months passed and Amanda gave birth to a lovely baby boy on the 19th July 2002, named Dylan. He was our first grandson. This was to change our approach to the business. How was Martin going to continue in the shop? What was he to do? Amanda was now a full-time mum, leaving Martin and Martine to run the shop.

It was a Monday night, 4th November 2002. Martin had just arrived home from the children's meeting which was held in Dromore Gospel Hall, Dromore, when he received a telephone call to say that his only brother, Dennis Beggs, had passed away. He was only fifty-two years of age. We will never forget the date as it was our youngest daughter Martine's birthday.

This really made me think. There I had been, some seven years previously, at death's door, but God had spared me through all my trials and troubles, yet here Dennis had been taken, as I would say, at a young age.

Haggai 1:7 says, "Thus saith the Lord of hosts; Consider your ways." As time is passing so quickly for everyone, I think it would be of benefit to us all to stop and think!

> Have you ever stopped to wonder
> What this life is all about?
> Why you're here and where you're going
> When your lease of time runs out?
> Maybe you've been far too busy,
> Trying hard to reach your goal!

Would you let me ask you kindly,
"Have you thought about your soul?"

You may reach your highest portals,
And your dreams may all come true;
Wealth and fame may be your portion,
And success may shine on you,
All your friends may sing your praises
Not a care on you may roll;
What about the Great Tomorrow -
Have you thought about your soul?

Don't forget your days are numbered,
Though you may be riding high;
But, like all of us poor mortals,
Someday you'll just up and die,
Your success and fame and glory
Won't be worth the bell they toll;
Let me ask you just one question,
"Have you thought about your soul?"

If you've never thought it over,
Spend a little time today;
There is nothing more important
That will ever come your way,
Than the joys of sins forgiven,
And to know you've been made whole;
In the name of Christ the Saviour,
Have you thought about your Soul?

Twin Tower Atrocity – 2001

One morning, in the month of September 2001, I switched
on my radio to listen to the news. A newsflash was broadcast
around the world that a terrorist attack had taken place in
the United States of America. Many lives were taken from
this scene of time into eternity with no warning given.

It was a lovely sunny morning that day, 11th September 2001, better known today as 'nine eleven'. Muslim extremists hijacked four planes and flew two of them into the building of the World Trade Centre in New York City, the third plane into the Pentagon and the fourth plane crashed in Pennsylvania. It emerged that passengers and crew had tried to regain control of the aircraft but tragedy struck.

We received a letter from our friends who were living in Blairstown, USA, the Rev. Walter and Diane Clarke, their son, Russell, and daughter, Heather. This is the family that we had the pleasure of having as guests for ten days some years previously. As I read this letter I was deeply touched, tears filled my eyes as I continued to read. Unknown to me, Russell Clarke was an employee with the World Trade Centre, USA and on that morning at 9:15am on September the eleventh he was due to be at work on the seventy-ninth floor of the second tower, but due to a mistake in his work calendar he believed he was to go there the following day instead.

Diane's last words were, "People are still scared that something else is going to happen, but we thank and praise God we still have our son, Russell." My thoughts were directed to that terrible scene and all those dear people who were caught up in this unpredictable situation, yet Russell had been preserved. What a separation took place that day in a moment. Many homes left without a father, mother, brother, sister etc.

My mind went directly to the word of God. What will it be like when an event occurs that Scripture tells is going to happen? It too will be sudden. In 1st Thessalonians 4 we read of Christ's return, the coming of the Lord. Verses 16 and 17 say, "For the Lord himself shall descend from Heaven with a shout, with the voice of the archangel, and with the trump of God: and the dead in Christ shall rise first; then we which are alive and remain shall be caught up together with them in the clouds, to meet the Lord in the air: and so shall we ever be with the Lord." It is only those who are ready – saved – who will respond to His voice and will arise. What a separation then! We read in Matthew 24 regarding this great event, verses 40-42 say, "Then shall two be in the field; the one shall be taken, and the other left. Two women shall be grinding at the mill; the one shall be taken, and the other left. Watch therefore: for ye know not what hour your Lord doth come." It is of the utmost importance, as we read in Amos 4:12, "Prepare to meet thy God." "Except ye repent," (of your sins to God), a warning is given - "ye shall all likewise perish." (Luke 13:3,5.)

Chapter 8

<u>Donaghcloney – Our Best Move</u>

After Martin's brother Dennis's funeral, I could see that Martin was feeling the strain of all that was happening. He needed help, so with much prayer we left all our problems with God to guide us in our next step forward.

At this time there was the big building boom; many were giving large sums of money for property, land and sites of old houses. Planning approval was being granted for nearly any site in the country. News soon got around that Martin was talking about retiring from business because once again I had to be admitted to hospital due to my illness. He was offered a price for the bungalow and the shop.

Martin and I talked things over and we decided to talk to an architect to consider planning permission for a number of houses which would be built on our ground at Ashfield. This was granted. We knew now this was the answer to prayer. We sold all and bought a house in Donaghcloney.

We were to leave Ashfield on the 4th October 2004. Many thoughts went through my mind. How would I settle into an environment with so many houses being built all around us? What would our neighbours be like - friendly, welcoming and sociable? Would they quickly adapt to my manner of speech using my servox? Would there be any disturbance from young children and from dogs barking continually? This was one thing that really annoyed me. Life would be so different now, living in a built-up area.

Bungalow, shop and yard up for sale

We got to know the builder of the housing development, who was called Henry. Henry was a Christian man and he had a great team of builders, joiners, electricians, painters etc. Many of these men were Christians and travelled from as far away as Kilkeel, outside Newcastle.

My daughter, Sharon, had been living with us at Ashfield with our granddaughter, Chloe. She was so cute and I loved her to bits. Chloe was just one of the family and Martine enjoyed the company, although she did not like to hear her cry. This was where the dummy came in handy! Sharon made the decision that she would rather start out in a house of her own. After much waiting and searching around for the right house, Sharon and Chloe finally settled into a new home not far from where we were going to reside in Donaghcloney. This was a big step for Sharon, after living with us for over thirty-five years and it was to leave me in a state of worry.

Our second grandson, Jack, was born on the 7th December 2004, a little baby brother for Dylan. At this stage we now had two grandsons and one granddaughter.

As Martin, Martine and I tried to settle into our new home we got to know the builders and, of course, many conversations and discussions took place, especially on the Scriptures, which I really enjoyed. By now these men were well aware of my situation because of the manner in which I spoke. I found them to be very sympathetic, caring and supportive in every way. Soon I was to be introduced to some of my neighbours. I found out that many of them were Christians. Truly the Lord was our guide. We could not have wished for any better.

Martine became very unsettled for some time and found it very hard to adjust to the area all around us. She would often say to her daddy and me, "I would rather be living up at Ashfield where I was born and brought up." Martine eventually settled into the new surroundings and got a wee job, working a few hours per week in the local shop in the village, known as Nisa shop. She got to know and love the staff members.

On the 11th November 2005 my eldest daughter, Pamela, gave birth to a baby boy called Jonathan. This was now our third grandson, our fourth grandchild. They were all to bring me much joy and pleasure.

My mother often said, "It's nice to see them coming, but it's also nice to see them leaving, especially when they are tired and get out of hand." This was very true in my situation.

More Invitations

Through time I was introduced to the Ulster Cancer Foundation at Eglantine Avenue, Belfast. It gave great support for all laryngectomy patients. My first invitation to this centre was to a laryngectomy conference. An ENT consultant was giving a talk on 'Living with Cancer'. Everything went well and I was able to concentrate on everything that was said. This was a very big help to me. But things were to change drastically for me. When I heard so many people speaking together, each using their artificial servox, I just felt I could not cope. I remember when I got home I went into a bout of depression. 'Is this what my voice is like?' I thought. I tried not to meditate or reflect back over the last few hours. It put me off attending such a conference for some considerable time.

The next invitation I received was to attend a conference on 'Living well with Cancer', which was to be held in the Wellington Park Hotel in Belfast. This was in the year of 2008. I had read in the newspaper about a well-known gentleman who had been a radio presenter with Downtown Radio, who had been diagnosed with throat cancer one year previously. His wife was a well- known figure in the media, a BBC journalist.

Their aim was to help others tackle such a disease and emphasis how vital it is for each one to listen to their bodies and to share any health concerns with their GP, no matter how trivial they think it may be. The word 'cancer' was always on my mind. Men in particular have a reluctance to speak openly about their health issues. I was really impressed with such a presentation given by them both. I got to know these two people as we had so much in common regarding health issues. We started to communicate with each other by letter writing, keeping each other informed of our daily progress. Once again, I was exercised to send a Bible, a few gospel tracts and a copy of my personal testimony to this couple and I received good feedback.

Amanda was now expecting her third baby. Alex Copeland was born on the 16th January 2011 but had some complications for which he required urgent attention. This gave me great concern, but again with the prayers of the Lord's dear people, Alex was well enough to return home to his mum, dad and brothers, Dylan and Jack.

The summertime soon came and all the gardens around us

were in bloom. The colours of all the different flowers were unbelievable. One Saturday afternoon, I was admiring the garden. Suddenly, I remembered about my two lovely blue pots which were sitting outside the conservatory door at the back of the house. I asked Martin to relocate them both to the front of our home.

The next day, after returning home from our Sunday morning remembrance meeting, held in the Gospel Hall in Dromore, I noticed something missing. Both my pots were gone. Someone had stolen them during the night while we slept in our beds. I became anxious just thinking that there was someone, or perhaps more than one person, out there watching our home.

I reported this theft to the police and I was given a space in our local newspaper, The Dromore Leader, to write a few words - a message of warning for all to be on their guard relating to the Donaghcloney/Craigavon area. This gave me an opportunity to bring another warning, a very solemn warning, which is found in the Bible, the word of God. Matthew 24:42-44 tells us, "Watch therefore: for ye know not what hour your Lord doth come. But know this, that if the goodman of the house had known in what watch the thief would come, he would have watched, and would not have suffered his house to be broken up. Therefore be ye also ready (meaning saved): for in such an hour as ye think not the Son of man cometh."

These solemn words that I had just written came forcibly before me. The Lord's return could take place at any moment. Was the Lord trying to establish in my mind that I had the gift of writing, as I could not speak? I knew that perhaps there were many people throughout the world who did not have a Bible and had never heard of gospel tracts and therefore did not realise the true meaning of Calvary or salvation. I finished my remarks by saying: "If anyone requires a Bible (King James Version) or gospel literature, free of charge, contact me at my address." The hymn below was dear to me and I used to sing it myself.

Go, labour on; spend, and be spent-
Thy joy to do the Father's will;
It is the way the Master went;
Should not the servant tread it still?

Go, labour on; 'tis not for nought;
Thine earthly loss is heavenly gain;
Men heed thee, love thee, praise thee not;
The Master praises - what are men?

Go, labour on; while it is day,
The world's dark night is hastening on;
Speed, speed thy work, cast sloth away,
It is not thus that souls are won.

Men die in darkness at your side,
Without a hope to cheer the tomb;
Take up the torch and wave it wide-
The torch that lights time's thickest gloom.

Toil on, faint not, keep watch and pray;
Be wise the erring soul to win;
Go forth into the world's highway,
Compel the wanderer to come in.

Toil on, and in thy toil rejoice!
For toil comes rest, for exile home;
Soon shalt thou hear the Bridegroom's voice,
The midnight cry: "Behold, I come!"

Horiatius Bonar (1808–89)

Matthew 9:37 came before me - "The harvest truly is

plenteous, but the labourers are few." This encouraged me to write my column for our weekly newspaper, relating to every day events in our society, bringing in the Scriptures from the word of God.

As time passed, I was approached by the editor, who asked if I would consider having an interview in my own home, in my own time, regarding my operation, my total loss of speech through cancer of the throat, and how I and my family had coped with the change. I hesitated as it was coming up to Christmas and I put it on hold at that time as I developed another chest infection.

As I started to get a little better and brighter, I made up my mind that if I was approached again by the same editor, I would consider it very carefully. It would mean being open and honest about my life to the general public. Would my story be a help and an encouragement to others who are passing through deep trials as the result of cancer? Sure enough, I was asked if I was up to the challenge. Eventually I gave in and said I would, but only on one condition - that I was allowed space to relate to all readers my story of how I came to know my sins forgiven through faith in Christ and in Him alone, and assurance of Heaven after death.

Arrangements were made and soon Martin and I were found sitting in our living room in Donaghcloney. I was very tearful as I sat beside the lady trying to relate to her my terrifying experience of finding out that I had throat cancer with the associated shock and the horror of it all. I told her that each of us take everything for granted. Our sleep, hearing, walking, taste and our voices are but a few examples. Losing my voice became a reality to me on the 26th June 1995. This lady spent some time in our home as I sought to relive my story as it happened. I finished my remarks by asking the lady to state that if any reader required a Bible (KJV), and gospel literature, free of charge, to contact me at my home address or contact telephone number. My story was published in our local paper the following week.

To my amazement, there was an overwhelming reaction. I received many letters to commend and praise me for the courage it took to record such an incredible story. I also received many requests for the KJV Bible and gospel tracts, from all denominations. What a joy it was for me to follow what God had set out before me.

Sometime later, I visited the town of Banbridge. When I walked into a shop, a lady came over to speak to me. She asked, "Are you the lady that writes the article that is printed in the paper?" I told her that yes, I was. She said to me, "Keep up the good work, because you never know who lifts the paper and reads your piece, which is so well presented, of how a sinner can come to know their sins forgiven." I can recall some days later that another lady approached me. She was a Christian and I knew right away, as she spoke to me, that she was very anxious about her son, who was out in the world enjoying the pleasures of sin, which are only 'for a season'. I got his name and address.

A few days passed and my mind was drawn to this young man and the heartbroken mother who watched her son who was not yet saved. I was pleased to send a KJV Bible with his name inscribed on it as well as a selection of gospel tracts relating to how a soul can be delivered from the power of Satan and be saved through faith in the Lord Jesus Christ.

Something I always did when I was posting any gospel literature was to send it recorded delivery. One Sunday afternoon we had just finished our dinner and were about to take a rest in our living room when our doorbell rang. Martin went to the door and opened it. There stood a young man with a little child and a bag in his hand. I heard the strange voice talking to Martin and, like any other woman, my nose got the better of me! I went to investigate as I heard my name being spoken - "Is Myrtle in?" Oh dear! What had I done?

I had never seen this young man before. He introduced himself to me stating that he was the person who had received the

Bible that I had sent. He told me that he had just got saved. Tears started to fill my eyes and just then he gave me a big hug and handed me a little box and said, "This is for you, Myrtle." I took it from him and said, "Thank you." He stayed for some time as Martin and he got into conversation.

After they both left, I opened the little box. It contained a small blossom bucket that contained two small plants, a spade and a fork as well as a small piece of carved wood with a lovely verse of Scripture inscribed on it. Here is what it said - "With God all things are possible" (Matthew 19:26).

This gave me great encouragement and the verse sits in my kitchen window for everyone to see and read. Luke 15:7 tells us, "I say unto you, that likewise joy shall be in Heaven over one sinner that repenteth, more than over ninety and nine just persons, which need no repentance." The lesson here is very clear, there is joy in Heaven over one sinner who repents, but there is no joy over the ninety and nine sinners who have never been convicted of their lost condition. This verse does not actually mean that there are some people who need no repentance. All men, women, boys and girls are sinners and all must repent in order to be saved.

Sometime later I had the great joy of sending this dear young man's partner a Bible with her name inscribed in it.

David Cameron (Son Ivan's Death)

In the month of March 2009, news came on air that our Prime Minister, Mr David Cameron, and his dear wife, Samantha, had a death in their family. Their son, Ivan, only six years of age, had passed away suddenly. I knew that Ivan had been born with a disability, but I was deeply shocked when I heard of his passing.

I was exercised to send my condolences to them, assuring

them of my thoughts and prayers at this very sad time of bereavement. I also brought them the word of God and explained that God our Saviour was in full control of all our lives. He saw fit to take Ivan home to be with Himself in Heaven. Ivan had no more pain and no more suffering now that he was at peace with God.

A lovely chorus came before me, one that I had learned in my young days while attending Sunday school and I knew that it would be some comfort to them both:

> There's a Friend for little children
> Above the bright blue sky;
> A Friend who never changeth,
> Whose love can never die.
> Unlike our friends by nature,
> Who change with changing years,
> This Friend is always worthy
> The precious name He bears.
>
> There's a home for little children,
> Above the bright blue sky;
> Where Jesus dwells in glory,
> A home of peace and joy.
> No home on earth is like it,
> Nor can with it compare;
> For everyone is happy,
> Nor could be happier there.
>
> There's a crown for little children,
> Above the bright blue sky -
> And all who look for Jesus,
> Shall wear it by and by.
> A crown of brightest glory,
> Which He will then bestow
> On all who trust the Saviour,
> And love His name below.

(Albert Midlane (1825-1909)

Sometime later I received a letter from David Cameron and his dear wife, Samantha, thanking me for my support and beautiful words in their deepest trial. There was enclosed in the envelope a lovely portrait of both David and Samantha and their new baby, not long born. Today, it sits on the hearth of our sitting room for all my visitors to see.

Stormont Visit

I, like many others, love to get invitations to go to special events, such as weddings, birthdays, garden and graduation parties. It was now January 2010 and the annual conference of the yearly laryngectomy talks was soon to take place. When I received my invitation, to my surprise I saw that it was to be held up in the Stormont building. I knew this is where all the MLAs (Members of Legislative Assembly) meet to discuss our future in this lovely country of ours, which is part of the United Kingdom. Neither Martin nor I had ever had the privilege of being invited to this great building. Would this be a golden opportunity for me to get the message of the gospel into Stormont?

The spokesperson at the conference was one of our MLAs. We were told we would be given a guided tour around some of the internal building before we separated later in the afternoon. When Martin and I entered the building and saw the hallway, my first reaction was, "Oh, my!" What a place! The massive chandeliers were beaming so brightly and the floors were sparkling. The stairway leading up to so many rooms looked fit for a king and queen. I had never entered or seen inside such a place before.

As we continued our guided tour around some of the main rooms, we eventually came to the one where all the MLAs sit. As I walked around, looking at all the names of our politicians and where they were seated, my eyes got a glimpse of the beautiful big armchair where the man in charge sat to command, "Order! Order, please!" to those who would seek to disrupt or disturb a meeting. My mind was directed to the Great Judgement Day when God will pass sentence on each unrepentant sinner. The Great White Throne is set. The Judge is seated; angels and archangels are in attendance. All heaven assembles with unnumbered millions and in breathless wonder survey the fearful scene with awe on every face as they wait. Time's final drama is to be enacted. Nothing else matters now. Everything of a secondary nature has been forgotten.

Presently, amid the awful silence, the dead appear, sinners great and small from every clime and race, sinners of the deepest dye along with those who have neglected and forgotten God. Books will be opened. The Book of Life is seen here. Revelation 20:15 reads, "And whosoever was not found written in the book of life was cast into the lake of fire." As I pondered this over in my mind, I thought to myself, What is it going to be like when this event takes place? That scene in that room has stayed with me until now. Another hymn comes to my mind. Just think of the words:

Have you thought of the great judgement day, sinner,
Of One who will sit on His throne,
From whose face Heaven and earth flee away sinner,
While you stand before Him alone.
No shelter for you will there be, sinner,
From Him who as Judge sitteth there,
No place whereto you may flee, sinner,
O, how will you shrink in despair.

All the dead, small and great, on that day, sinner,
From earth and from sea shall arise.
Death and hell cannot hold back their prey, sinner,
Nor hide the lost souls from His eyes.
Your sins you will meet on that day, sinner,
The books shall your record unfold;
No prayer will that guilt wash away, sinner,
No ransom or silver or gold.

In the Lamb's book of life on that day, sinner,
Your name will be sought for in vain;
To the dread lake of fire cast away, sinner,
For ever you'll linger in pain;
Unless in the day of His grace, sinner,
You trust in the Christ who has died,
Who suffered for sin, in your place, sinner,
On Calvary's tree crucified.

William Rodgers (1879-1951)

Just before we separated, I had the great privilege of handing over to the spokesman (MLA) a Bible, a letter, a few gospel tracts and a script of my own personal testimony to be left in the library for anyone to read.

A Terrifying Experience

A few weeks before Christmas 2011, I became so unwell that my family had to call the out-of-hours doctor. Straight away, after the doctor examined me, an ambulance was called to transport me to the nearest A&E (Accident and Emergency) Department. Arriving at this department can be very traumatic and disturbing and I became very anxious, fearing the unknown as so much can happen all around us in a short space of time.

As I lay in that bed, waiting to see a doctor, I was very aware of what was going on around me. There was so much pressure on our doctors, nurses, office staff, porters etc. Telephones were ringing; doctor's beepers were going off. I could hear a nurse saying continually, "Another transfer to Ward A...another patient ready for admission...so and so is going home...two more patients transferred up to the ward, to two South..."

Soon I was given a transfer to a ward to continue my treatment. I thought, 'Great, I will get away from all the turmoil.' I was given a wee ward of my own. However, a lady in the single ward opposite mine became distraught. All I could hear from her lips was, "Let me out of here, I want out." In all my weakness I heard these words from her lips continuously. I really felt sorry for this dear lady as I learned later that her medication was restricted because of certain tests being carried out. This continued on for some time and her words struck terror to me. My thoughts were directed to that awful place called Hell.

John 3:36 makes it very clear. Those who reject God's only Son, Jesus Christ, and refuse to accept Him as their own and personal Saviour, the wrath of God will abide on him. How sad, but how solemn. No escape, and it will be for all eternity.

I became confused in my own mind. I could not even think straight. I started to cry, tears streaming down my cheeks. I lifted my servox to speak, but it wasn't working either. What a state I got myself into. Just at this point I reached for my 'sword' that I had brought with me - my Bible - and opened it at Revelation 2:10 - "Fear none of those things which thou shalt suffer: behold, the devil shall cast some of you into prison, that ye may be tried." Deuteronomy 33:27 says, "The eternal God is thy refuge, and underneath are the everlasting arms." With my Bible opened my tears soon dried up. A nurse came over to me. I lifted my servox out of the charger and was able to testify to her that I had a friend (my Saviour) who 'sticketh closer than a brother'. I could see the tears in her eyes. She said, "It must be hard," and I nodded my head. Yes, I knew that the Lord was in full control. I was saved forty-five years previously at 1:05am on the 21st November 1966. I had accepted the Lord Jesus Christ as my own and personal Saviour.

My condition started to improve. A few days before I was to be discharged from hospital, my consultant came to see me to ask if I would have any objection to him bringing some student doctors to have a talk with me about my throat cancer and perhaps give them an outline of my medical history, both before and after my operation. I had no time to think properly, so I agreed with the doctor's request.

The next day, sure enough, I was surrounded by a team of eight or nine student doctors, both young men and women. I had never met any one of these students before, nor did I know their background, their religion or what county or country they came from. I treated each and every one of them equally.

After my consultant introduced me to the students I felt very relaxed. I was able to tell them, lifting my servox, something about the device I was holding in my hand and how it worked. The students were impressed by the sound of my words being expressed out of my mouth just at the press of a button. Some could understand quite well what I was saying; others took some time to get used to such a device. I was able to tell them something of my history before my operation and how I felt when I was told I had throat cancer.

I told them that my first reaction was, 'I'm going to die!' After I explained the effects it had on my family, I could see some of these young men and women becoming emotional. Then I offered my words to them of a brighter future that lies before me. I was able to tell them of God's love to me, how that we were all sinners. I referred to those verses in Romans 3:22-23 - "For there is no difference: for all have sinned, and come short of the glory of God." I was able to relate to them, as they stood around my bed, how I had come to know Christ as my Saviour. Before they left me, each one had a look at my device and thought it was amazing. They thanked me for allowing them to hear some of my incredible story and said my positive attitude was great. Soon I was well enough to go home to my family and friends.

Queen's Diamond Jubilee (1952 – 2012)

The 27th June 2012 was a great day for many of thousands of people. A garden party had been arranged at the Stormont Estate in Belfast. This was a celebration of the Queen's Diamond Jubilee, sixty years wearing the crown of jewels.

Martin, Sharon, Chloe and I had the great privilege of attending as guests. The weather was beautiful and the sight of so many people waving the flag to greet the Queen and Prince Philip was unbelievable. Everyone was so excited just to get a glimpse of Her Majesty Queen Elizabeth II. I can remember seeing Her Majesty as she passed us in the limousine with Prince Philip, waving her hand and giving us a lovely smile.

Photo of us at the Queen's Diamond Jubilee (1952-2012)

At the Queen's Diamond Jubilee (1952-2012)

The cheers and clapping of hands were heard from all around. It was at this point I felt alone, isolated, separated from everyone, even my family. Eventually, when I returned home my mind started to travel back over what I had witnessed throughout the day. There was so much planning for such an event with so much security all around to ensure that everything passed off peacefully.

My thoughts went directly to the word of God. Again we read of our Saviour, the Lord Jesus Christ, laid in a manager and made lower than the angels. Christ's priesthood became us (Hebrews 7:26). He was holy in

His standing before God. He was harmless and guileless in His dealings with men. He was undefiled in His personal character. He was separate from sinners in His life. He became higher than the Heavens.

Let's trace His path. He descends from Heaven to Bethlehem to Gethsemane to Golgotha to the tomb. The gospels tell us that Christ arose and after forty days He ascended unto His Father in Heaven, not only a Prince, but a Saviour. Mark the stages of His humiliation – at the age of thirty-three and half years, Christ knew He was to wear a crown on this earth, but not a crown of royalty. Matthew 27:29 tells us that a crown of twisted thorns was placed and pressed on His head and a reed was placed in His right hand. What suffering my Saviour had to endure as He hung upon that cruel cross of Calvary. People mocked Him, spat on His lovely face, plucked the hair from off His cheeks. Luke 22:44 tells us, "His sweat was as it were great drops of blood falling down to the ground." The pain, suffering and agony for six hours on the cross of Calvary was in God's gracious purpose that Christ might taste death for everyone. This includes you and me.

What a total isolation our Saviour endured. He bore it patiently throughout His time of both physical and mental suffering on the cross of Calvary. Christ wore the crown as our substitute.

For sixty years Her Majesty Queen Elizabeth II has worn a crown of jewels. My Saviour wore a crown of thorns for six hours in agony and cried out, "It is finished." The work was complete. He will not wear the crown of thorns again.

Our grandchildren L to R Front:
Jack, Chloe with Alex, Dylan, back Jonathan

Epilogue

As I cast my mind back over the last number of years I can see how God has guided me and has given me strength and a clear mind to be able to concentrate on putting words together, to compile letters to many celebrities, especially those who have lost a loved one through such an illness as mine.

I have been able to distribute many letters, gospel literature and KJV Bibles to each of the Royal family. The response has been very encouraging. I can say in truth, 'To God be the glory, great things He hath done!' He has brought me through so many trials and disappointments in my life.

"For your Father knoweth what things ye have need of, before ye ask him" (Matthew 6:8).

"I can do all things through Christ which strengtheneth me" (Philippians 4:13).

My Voice Tells The Story